BrightRED Results

Standard Grade
MODERN STUDIES

Graeme Glen

BrightRED
PUBLISHING

First published in 2010 by:

Bright Red Publishing Ltd
6 Stafford Street
Edinburgh
EH3 7AU

Copyright © Bright Red Publishing Ltd 2010

Cover image © Caleb Rutherford

All rights reserved. No part of this publication may be reproduced, stored in a retrieval system, or transmitted in any form or by any means, electronic, mechanical, photocopying, recording or otherwise, without prior permission in writing from the publisher.

The right of Graeme Glen to be identified as the author of this work has been asserted by him in accordance with sections 77 and 78 of the Copyright, Designs and Patents Act 1988.

A CIP record for this book is available from the British Library

ISBN 978-1-906736-17-0

With thanks to Ken Vail Graphic Design, Cambridge (layout) and Roda Morrison (copy-edit)

Cover design by Caleb Rutherford-eidetic

Illustrations by Beehive illustration (Martin Sanders) and Ken Vail Graphic Design, Cambridge.

Acknowledgements

The author would like to thank all those who have helped and supported him throughout the writing of this book.

Every effort has been made to seek all copyright holders. If any have been overlooked then Bright Red Publishing will be delighted to make the necessary arrangements.

Bright Red Publishing would like to thank the Scottish Qualifications Authority for use of Past Exam Questions. Answers do not emanate from SQA.

Photo © Jeff J Mitchell/Getty Images News/Getty Images (page 18); Photo © Andrew JW/Creative Commons* (page 18); Photo © Jeff J Mitchell/Getty Images News/Getty Images (page 21); Photo © Jeff J Mitchell/Getty Images News/Getty Images (page 23); Photo © Jeff J Mitchell/Getty Images News/Getty Images (page 28); Photo © Jeff J Mitchell/Getty Images News/Getty Images (page 29); Logo © Greenpeace (page 34); Photo © PAUL ELLIS/AFP/Getty Images (page 36); Photo © International Rivers/Creative Commons* (page 36); Photo © Jenny Downing/Creative Commons* (page 39); Photo © David Rayner/Creative Commons* (page 40); Photo © Color Day Production/Stone/Getty Images (page 41); Logos © Age Concern and Help the Aged (page 48); New Deal logo © Department for Work & Pensions (page 58); EMA logo © Learning and Skills Council (page 58); SureStart logo © Department for Children, Schools and Families (page 58); Logo © Child Trust Fund (page 58); Logos for Skillseekers and Modern Apprenticeships © Skills Development Scotland (page 65); Logos for New Deal and Jobcentreplus © Department of Work & Pensions (page 65); EMA Logo © Learning and Skills Council (page 65); Photo © David Paul Morris/Getty Images News/Getty Images (page 71); Photo © Jason Squires/WireImage/Getty Images (page 74); Photo © Reinhold Matay/WireImage/Getty Images (page 75); Photo © Alex Wong/Getty Images News/Getty Images (page 77); Photo © Rob Tringali/SportsChrome/Getty Images (page 82); Photo © Siri Stafford/Taxi/Getty Images (page 83); Photo © Tony Hutchings/Stone/Getty Images (page 83); Photo © Mel Yates/Taxi/Getty Images (page 85); Logo © UNICEF (page 91); Photo © WFP/Stephanie Savariaud (page 92); Logo © UNESCO (page 93); Logo © International Labour Organization (page 93); Logo © NATO (page 103); Logo © EuropeanCommunities (page 103); Photo © SHAH MARAI/AFP/Getty Images (page 108).

* Licensed under the Creative Commons Attribution-Share Alike 2.0 Generic license. Details can be viewed at: http://creativecommons.org/licenses/by-sa/2.0/deed.en

Contents

Introduction			2
Chapter	1	**The exam**	4
Chapter	2	**Modern Studies – concepts and key words**	6
Chapter	3	**Writing skills in Modern Studies**	9
Chapter	4	**Living in a Democracy**	13
		British politics	13
		Trade unions	28
		Pressure groups	34
Chapter	5	**Changing Society**	39
		The elderly	39
		The family	51
		Employment	59
Chapter	6	**Ideologies – the USA**	69
Chapter	7	**International Relations**	90
		Politics of aid	90
		Alliances	103
Chapter	8	**Enquiry Skills**	115
Chapter	9	**Conclusion**	140

Introduction

Revising for your exam

What is Standard Grade Modern Studies?

Standard Grade is a two-year Modern Studies course that is usually spread over third and fourth year of your secondary schooling. It will result in either a Credit, General or Foundation award. To gain a Credit you must gain a grade 1 or 2, General requires you to gain a 3 or 4 and Foundation is a grade 5 or 6 award.

If you want to achieve to the best of your ability (or beyond!) and obtain a good grade, so you can advance to your Intermediate or Higher course, then this is definitely the book for you!

The importance of Modern Studies

Modern Studies is becoming a very important subject, not just in schools, but in everyday life and the wider world. It is vital today to have an understanding of complex world issues, such as international terrorism, conflict, war, famine and increasing unemployment (to name just a few), to know what causes them and, more importantly, how they can be addressed. It is equally important to have an understanding of the political, social and economic issues we face as a society here in the UK. Standard Grade Modern Studies teaches you the key knowledge and evaluating skills you require to understand these wide ranging issues.

You will learn many skills in Modern Studies:

- How to develop your knowledge and understanding of concepts
- How to develop your responses to questions, so that you gain the most from your answer
- How to use sources of information to analyse a question
- Structuring an essay/response
- Developing perspectives and balance in your arguments
- An awareness of the wider world and its issues

Introduction

The Modern Studies syllabus

The Modern Studies course is very detailed. There are four syllabus areas with a total of nine sections (topics) to study. You **MUST** have a good level of knowledge of the course in order to effectively use the skills outlined previously. If you have this and you follow the advice in the following pages, you have every chance of success in Standard Grade Modern Studies!

The syllabus areas and topics you will study are:

Area 1   **Living In a Democracy**
(British Politics, Trade Unions, Pressure Groups)

Area 2   **Changing Society**
(The Elderly, The Family, Employment)

Area 3   **Ideologies**
(The USA, China. Note you will only study **1** ideology)

Area 4   **International Relations**
(Politics of Aid, Alliances)

All areas can be examined at both General and Credit level. There is no set routine for which topics will appear. In other words an elderly knowledge and understanding (KU) question could appear in both the general and credit papers for the same year. This means **you** have to be very well prepared at KU level.

Course assessment

Unlike other subjects you may be studying, such as English, there is no internal assessment in Modern Studies. Your assessment **IS** your Standard Grade examination. It counts for all 100% of your grade. You will sit a prelim exam a few months before the final exam in order to help you prepare, and you may have a shorter exam after the first year of your Standard Grade course. Some schools might have syllabus area assessments at the end of a unit, to see how well you understood it. But you are always working towards the final exam. That is why it is so important to prepare throughout the two years of your Standard Grade course. You wouldn't turn up to run a 26 mile marathon without training first, would you?!

How this book will help you

This book will take you through the course. It will cover all four syllabus areas and the topics included in each one. As we go through the book, there will be some knowledge included to remind you of key concepts and areas you will have studied and revised. However, this is not simply a revision book. This book is designed to help you produce the answer that will get you the best possible General or Credit pass. Any knowledge in the book is there to show you how you can use it to provide a Knowledge and Understanding answer. This book is all about you developing your answers in a simple but very effective way.

Although your Standard Grade course will run over two years, the most important year is the year leading up to your final examination (usually fourth year). This book will concentrate on the General and Credit skills you require to develop during fourth year. It will cover certain course content and the exam answer skills and techniques required.

Chapter 1 The exam

The exam

For most students the final exam will take place in May of fourth year. You will sit two papers. If your teacher and the evidence predict you are a Credit or a good General student, then you will sit the Credit and General papers. If, however, you are just doing okay at General or you are a Foundation pupil, then you will sit the General and Foundation papers.

The Credit paper lasts 2 hours, the General paper 1 hour and 30 minutes and the Foundation paper is 1 hour. Base the time you give to each answer on the length of time you have. A good way to judge timings is to divide the length of time by the number of syllabus areas. For example, the Credit paper lasts 120 minutes. Divide this by the 4 syllabus areas, giving you 30 minutes per area for answering. Likewise, General lasts 90 minutes, giving you approximately 22 minutes per syllabus area.

The balance of the paper is very important. In all papers you answer, Knowledge and Understanding (KU) counts for 40% of the (question) marks and Enquiry Skills (ES) counts for the other 60% of the (question) marks.

To gain the higher grade in the paper you should aim for 70–75% or higher of the marks, so if the KU section was out of 32 marks you must gain 24 marks or more and if the ES section was out of 40 marks, you would need 30 marks or more.

The lower grade in the paper is between 50% and 70%.

Below 50% for a paper results in a grade 7 (fail) for that paper.

Because the Enquiry Skills section has more marks awarded to it, the ES grade is the dominant factor in your final grade. For example:

You receive 32 marks out of 32 for your KU in the Credit paper. This is 100% and a grade 1. However, if you receive 24 out of 40 marks in the ES section, this is 60% and therefore a grade 2. This means your final grades are KU 1 and ES 2. As we have seen, because Enquiry Skills has a greater chunk of the marks, the balance goes towards it. This means you would end up with an overall grade 2.

Look out for

These are opinion scores. Aim for a higher %.

Be aware!

There are a number of important issues to look out for in a Modern Studies exam paper.

In a General paper every Knowledge and Understanding (KU) and Enquiry Skills (ES) question is worth **4** marks. (The only question that is not is the investigating question.)

A General question will also tell you how many answer parts you need to provide. It is always **two**.

In KU questions at General level you can be awarded up to **3** marks for one answer if it is really good. A not so good second answer might only get **1** mark but the candidate still gets 4/4 full credit. The same applies to KU at Credit.

In a Credit paper, however, it is a little different.

KU and ES questions will be worth either 4, 6, 8, or even 10 marks. (The 10 mark question will be an ES question.) Also, the question will not tell you how many answer parts to provide. You should however work on the basis that each answer part you give is worth 2 marks. Perhaps think of sticking to the idea of 2 marks per answer part. Therefore if the question is worth 8 marks, you need to give four paragraphed answers.

Chapter 2: Modern Studies – concepts and key words

Concepts

In Standard Grade Modern Studies, you will be introduced to various concepts. These concepts are found in the Knowledge and Understanding section of the course. A concept is a belief or idea of something. If you can understand the concept involved in the particular work you are studying, it should make it easier to understand and answer the KU question.

concept: *noun* an abstract or general idea derived from particular instances

The key concepts introduced/covered in Modern Studies are:

- Representation: Acting, speaking or making decisions on behalf of others, e.g. class captain, shop steward.
- Rights and Responsibilities: Freedoms and choices we have and the duties that accompany them, e.g. the right to vote and the responsibility to vote sensibly.
- Equality: Having the same level of status or wealth as another, e.g. some single parent families have a lower living standard than other families.
- Participation: Joining in, taking part, becoming involved, e.g. Barack Obama standing as a Presidential candidate.
- Ideology: Ideas and beliefs about a political or economic system, e.g. the UK is a democratic system.
- Need: What people must have in order to survive and progress, e.g. some argue the Government does not fully meet the needs of the unemployed.
- Power: Methods or tactics countries or people use to defend themselves or to exert influence over others, e.g. giving tied aid to a developing nation.

! Look out for

You will see the concept box above each section of revision throughout this book.

Key words

You will also meet many new words and phrases in Standard Grade Modern Studies.

The main exam phrases you will hear are Knowledge and Understanding (KU) and Enquiry Skills (ES).

Knowledge and Understanding

Knowledge and Understanding questions will take the following styles:

- **Describe**, which means **tell me** what happens or what is done. An example could be to describe ways in which people can take part in politics. One way could be by voting.

- **Give reasons**, which means **tell me why** something happens or is done. An example could be to give reasons why some Americans are worse off than others in terms of education.

- **Explain**, which means **tell me how** and **why** something happens or is done, i.e. you have to describe and give reasons. An example could be to explain the advantages of a worker joining a trade union. You cannot explain the advantages without describing what they are. Your answer could be: if you are a trade union member you will be represented over pay levels.

For Reference: For ease of understanding we will refer to all answer paragraphs as **arguments**. For example, if the question asks you to 'give two reasons' or 'describe ways in which', we will discuss the answer paragraphs as **arguments**.

Be aware!

One thing you should be aware of is the inclusion over the last few years of drawings in the KU questions, especially at General level. These drawings have been put in by the SQA exam team to help give the candidate ideas for them to use as responses. However, you can include arguments/ideas of your own. The drawings are not a complete list. Because these types of questions have proved to be helpful, they will continue to be included in future years.

Enquiry Skills

Enquiry Skills questions will ask you to answer, based on sources. The sources found in the Credit exam paper are more detailed and complex than those at General level!

General

ES General questions will take the following styles:

- **Differences:** You will be asked to give differences in the information between sources.
- **Option choice:** You will be asked to choose the best option out of two, based on information in the sources.
- **Support/oppose:** You will be asked to give reasons to support or oppose. This means the same as agree or disagree with, be for or against what someone says, based on the information in the source.

continued

Chapter 2 Modern Studies – concepts and key words

- **Exaggeration:** You will be asked to show how a statement made by someone is exaggerated, based on the information in the source. The word exaggerate means to overstate, take beyond the truth, stretch the truth or potentially be wrong.

- **Conclusion:** Based on the information in the sources you will be asked to reach conclusions about different issues. They could range from the number of questions asked in Parliament to how much different countries spend on their armed forces. The word conclusion means a result. You will need to come to a decision or reach a judgement on something.

- **Investigating:** This is when you are asked to suggest ways of carrying out an investigation.

Credit

ES Credit questions will take the following styles:

- **Selective in the use of facts:** Based on the information in the sources you must identify evidence that is truthful (right) and/or incorrect (wrong). Usually you will do this based on a statement made by a person. You must also state how far the person is being selective.

- **Support/oppose:** See the list for General on previous page.

- **Conclusion:** See the list for General, above.

- **Option choice/decision making:** See the list for General on previous page.

- **Hypothesis:** You are given a topic to investigate and you must give a statement relevant to that topic that you can prove or disprove.

The main difference in ES questions at Credit level is the sources are greater in number and more detailed in their information. Make sure you respond appropriately to the depth of detail in the sources.

Writing skills in Modern Studies — Chapter 3

Importance of writing skills

What you should know…

Providing correctly structured answers in Modern Studies is a vital part of gaining examination success. You may have all the knowledge and understanding in the world, and you may be able to identify relevant source information, but if you can't produce your written answer correctly then it will be more difficult for you to gain the grade your hard work deserves.

Make sure you include the basic skills of good writing in your answers. You know – those you learned at primary school, but forgot when you arrived at secondary!!

- Capital letters at the start of a sentence.
- Answer in sentences. A paragraph is not one long sentence!
- Include commas and full stops.
- Include joining words and phrases in your answer, such as: therefore, however, an additional reason, as well as, a further way.
- Answers should be paragraphed. Each reason you give should have its own paragraph. This means if the question asks you to give **two** reasons, you should produce **two** paragraphs, i.e. one paragraph for each reason.

These skills are the basic starting blocks for an effective Standard Grade answer. However, there are additional ways you can improve your answer.

In Standard Grade Credit Modern Studies classes you may use a method called **PEER**. This stands for:

POINT: You give your point/reason/way.

EXPLAIN: You explain the meaning of the point/reason/way.

EXAMPLE: You give an example to back up the explanation.

RELATE: You show how the example relates back to the original point you made.

It is a bit like going all the way round a clock. You begin at 12 o'clock and travel all the way round, arriving back at 12 o'clock!

This is a method you should get into the habit of practising. So, if you have to provide two reasons why women are under-represented in the House of Commons, you must PEER twice: once for each reason.

PEER is a method you should use when answering Credit Knowledge and Understanding questions.

*At General level you use the exact same method **apart** from the **RELATE**. So you just PEE!*

When you are practising answering General questions you should start by just using PEE: Point, Explain, Example. This is an easier way of understanding the method. However, when you move on to Credit questions you should add the R for Relate to your answer.

Chapter 3 Writing skills in Modern Studies

Example answers

So here are two example paragraph answers. The first paragraph is a PEE answer to a General question, the second a PEER answer to a Credit question.

Something to notice!

Where answers are provided throughout the book, you will see that the paragraph has different colours included in it. This is a colour coding system to help you understand the PEE and PEER methods. The colours stand for:

BLACK = The POINT being made

GREEN = The EXPLANATION of the point

VIOLET = The EXAMPLE given

BLACK = RELATE to show how the example proves the point

General example (PEE)

General question

> People should use their **right** to vote.
>
> Give **two** reasons why people should use their **right** to vote.
>
> (KU, 4 marks)

In the example answer below, only one paragraph has been given. But remember – the question asks for two reasons, so you would have to provide a second paragraph.

General – answer

There are a number of reasons why people should use their right to vote. (POINT) *One reason is that in the United Kingdom it is a democratic right that people have.* (EXPLAIN) *This means that a person has the right to do as they wish providing it is within the law, such as voting for whichever candidate they want in their constituency.* (EXAMPLE) *For example, a person in the Clydebank and Milngavie constituency could vote for Des McNulty if they wanted him to be their MSP.*

Can you see where each part of PEE is, in the answer?

POINT (Sentence 2)

EXPLAIN (Sentence 3)

EXAMPLE (Sentence 4)

10

Credit example (PEER)

Credit question

> American citizens can **participate** in politics in many ways.
>
> Describe, **in detail**, the ways in which American citizens can **participate** in politics.
>
> (KU, 8 marks)

In the answer below, one paragraph has been given as an example. But remember the question is for **8 marks**, so you should give at least three but probably four ways in which American citizens can participate in politics.

Credit – answer

There are many ways citizens of the United States can participate in politics. (POINT) One such way is to join and become a member of a Political Party. (EXPLAIN) This is when, if they have an interest in politics, they may join a party and become involved in the work of the party. (EXAMPLE) For example, a citizen may join the Republican or Democratic Party, as current President Obama once did. Once a member they can attend party meetings and rallies and vote on party decisions. During an election campaign they may become involved in handing out leaflets or putting up posters for example. (RELATE) This shows by having this interest in politics, an American citizen can participate in the work of their political party and play a role in the political process of their country.

Can you see where each part of PEER is, in the answer?

- POINT (Sentence 2)
- EXPLAIN (Sentence 3)
- EXAMPLE (Sentence 4, 5, 6)
- RELATE (Sentence 7)

Writing a paragraph is when you join your Point, Explanation, Example and RELATE all together. One such way to do this for the above question could be: (POINT) 'One way an American citizen can participate is ...' (EXPLAIN) 'This means that ...' (EXAMPLE) 'For example ...' (RELATE) 'This shows that ...'

Your turn!

Hopefully you can see this is a relatively simple method to use. If you use this method, it should get you the necessary marks. Although the Credit question above about participating in American politics was worth 8 marks, you should aim to get full marks using the PEER method. You know you could think of another three ways of participating!

- Vote
- Stand as a candidate
- Join an interest group

Try to complete both the General and Credit questions we have just looked at.

continued

Chapter 3 Writing skills in Modern Studies

Include the following steps in your work:

- Read the question carefully, understanding what you are being asked, the number of marks and the concept.
- Give your argument.
- Explain the argument.
- Give an example to back up the argument and explanation.
- Provide a relationship, showing how the example highlights the point as an argument.

Remember to PEE for General and PEER for Credit!!

Explaining the answer: Knowledge and Understanding

When you read the text below you will notice that the paragraphs include sections that are different colours. This is to help you distinguish each part of your answer.

Remember, your General KU answer should be based on: Point – Explain – Example!

But at Credit level it should be: Point – Explain – Example – Relate!

The first part of your answer, which we have illustrated in black, is the point. This is when you give your reason or method. For example, if you are asked to describe one way in which the United Nations meets the needs of people in Africa, you would give a description of this. You could include information such as Unicef helping to meet their needs.

The second section, which we have illustrated in green, is when you explain what the organisation of Unicef does in order to help meet the needs. This could be by providing education and immunisation programmes for children.

The third section, which we have illustrated in violet, gives the example of Unicef at work. An example could be that they have established immunisation programmes for 1·5 million mothers and children against measles in Rwanda.

The fourth section, which we have illustrated in black, is the 'relate' part. This is when you connect back to the original point. For example you could say: 'This example clearly shows how Unicef, as part of the United Nations has a major role in helping to meet the needs of people in Africa through its many programmes such as immunisation.' In this way, you go full circle back to the beginning!

If you base your answer on this principle, you will have answered all areas of the question. **Remember** though that if the question is for 4 marks, you must carry out Point – Explain – Example – Relate twice in the answer. You should work on the basis that each argument, reason, or description you give is worth 2 marks. So if it's an 8 mark question you need to PEER 4 times!!

Living in a Democracy — Chapter 4

British politics

What you should know…

There are six key areas you can be questioned on at General and/or Credit level in relation to British politics in Living in a Democracy:

- Reasons why it is important to vote in elections.
- Ways people can participate in election campaigns.
- Ways in which MPs/MSPs represent constituents.
- Rights of citizens when opposing new laws.
- Reasons why specific groups are under-represented in Parliament.
- Advantages and disadvantages of certain voting systems.

Reasons why voting is important

What you should know…

> The concept being assessed is **rights and responsibilities**.
> *To exercise the freedoms and choices we have.*

An area you can be questioned on at General and Credit Knowledge and Understanding (KU) levels, is 'the reasons why people should use their right to vote'.

We have provided below a recap summary to remind you of the main reasons. Afterwards there are example General and Credit KU questions and sample answers.

Summary

- Voting is a democratic right that people have in the UK. Many countries don't have this right, therefore people believe citizens should use the right if they have it. People fought for this democratic right. Voters today should respect this sacrifice.
- It is argued that if you don't vote for the people who represent you in Parliament, then you don't have any right to criticise the decisions they make.
- People who work pay tax to the Government. This tax money pays for services we use, such as education, transport, etc. Don't you think the people who pay this tax should have a say on how it is spent? They won't if they don't vote!
- If people don't vote this can lead to a low voter turnout, say less than 50%. This means whoever becomes the governing political party was chosen by less than half the country. However, this party will be making decisions for the whole country. Vote and you may get the party you want in power!
- If people do not vote it might allow extremist parties to gain some power. This can allow them to influence decisions in ways the majority do not want.
- Any other valid point. (Be aware that this is not a complete list. You may think of other possible ideas and examples yourself. Look at www.parliament.uk.)

Chapter 4 Living in a Democracy

General question (2002 Q1c)

> People should use their **right** to vote.
>
> Give **two** reasons why people should use their **right** to vote.
>
> (KU, 4 marks)

Look out for

How many reasons does the question ask for? Stick to this!

General answer

One reason why people should use their right to vote is, if you do not vote, it could be argued that you do not have a right to complain about the result or decisions made. This means that if you have not voted you cannot argue or complain about who becomes your elected MP or MSP. Also you do not have the right to be unhappy about decisions made in Parliament or by the Government. For example, if you did not vote and Des McNulty became your MSP, you do not have the right to complain about him becoming the representative for Clydebank and Milngavie.

A second reason why people should use their right to vote is that election results based on a low voter turnout are not always reliable. This means if not many people in the country go out to vote in an election, the country ends up with representatives or governments that most of the people may not have wanted. For example, if less than half the people living in East Dunbartonshire vote in a General Election and Jo Swinson from the Liberal Democrats wins, she might have done so with over 50% of the constituency not wanting her as an MP.

Look out for

Use the wording of the question to start your answer.

Look out for

Remember that the colours each stand for a different section of PEE!

Credit question (2006 Q1b)

> In a democracy, it is important that people use their right to vote.
>
> Explain, **in detail**, why it is important for people to use their right to vote.
>
> (KU, 4 marks)

Look out for

A Credit question will **not** tell you the number of reasons to give. You should refer to the number of marks as a guide.

Look out for

Although the General and Credit questions are worded differently, with the wording of the Credit question being a little more complicated, you should understand that they are asking the exact same thing: **Why should people vote?!**

Credit answer

It is important, in a democracy, that people use their right to vote for a number of reasons. One reason that could be argued is if you do not use your democratic right to vote, you have no right to complain about the representatives you have and the decisions they make. If you decide at an election you will not vote, you cannot criticise the candidate who wins the seat for your constituency. You would have no right to criticise decisions made by them. For example, if you live in the Edinburgh South West constituency, and you want the Conservative Party to win, if you do not use your right to vote, you have no right to complain if Alistair Darling of the Labour Party wins that constituency. Therefore if people wish to complain about the decisions that are reached it is important they use their right to vote.

A further reason why it is important for people to use their right to vote is Governments spend tax money collected from a large number of the electorate. This means that if the Government is spending people's money, they should get a say in how it is spent. The way to do this is to vote for the representative you want, who will express your views. For example, in early 2008, Northern Rock bank suffered financial problems. The Government gave the bank £55 billion in order to keep it open. By voting in General Elections for a representative, voters have a say whether or not the Government should help areas, such as banks. If you do not vote, you might not have the representative you may have wanted making those decisions for you.

Look out for

Remember that each colour stands for a different section of PEER!

Can you see the difference between a General and Credit answer? A General answer uses simpler wording. You make a simple point, give a brief explanation and then an example to back up the explanation. Your General answer will usually be shorter in length.

Your Credit answer will be more complex. Your point will be similar in style to General level. However, the explanation and example require more detail. (You should see this from the example above.) Remember too, that at Credit you must make sure you relate back to the original point.

Ways of participating in election campaigns

What you should know…

The concept being assessed is **participation**.
Ways people can take part in a democracy.

An area you can be questioned on at General and Credit KU levels is 'ways people can participate in election campaigns'.

We have provided below a recap summary to remind you of the main ways. Afterwards there are example General and Credit KU questions and sample answers.

continued

Chapter 4 Living in a Democracy

What you should know – continued

Summary

- Joining a political party, such as the Labour Party, the Conservative Party, etc. By joining, you increase their membership and this helps add to their power.
- Canvassing the electorate. This means you go to people's doors or telephone them to gain their opinion on issues or to find out who they are likely to vote for.
- Publicising the party. People find out information through publicity. Handing out leaflets to people and putting up posters gets a party noticed by the electorate.
- Helping to organise meetings. Candidates will hold meetings and events where the electorate can go along, ask questions and find out what the candidate will do if he/she is elected. These events need to be organised by helpers.
- Helping explain to people the process of voting. Some people may be put off voting as they are unsure what to do at the polling station where they vote. Volunteers are there to help them, by answering any questions people may have about voting or explaining how they carry out the process of voting.
- Providing transport on polling day. Some people may not be able to get to the polling station to vote. Parties provide transport for these people, such as the elderly. The elderly make up approximately 15% of the population. This is a lot of voters! Getting them out to vote may help a candidate win the constituency.
- Any other valid point. (Be aware that this is not a complete list. You may think of other possible ideas and examples yourself.)

Labour

www.labour.org.uk
www.libdems.org.uk
www.snp.org
www.conservatives.com
www.greenparty.org.uk

General question (2007 Q1a)

Describe **two** ways in which supporters of a candidate can help during an election campaign.

(KU, 4 marks)

Look out for

Make sure you read the wording of the question carefully.

General answer

One way in which supporters of a candidate can help during an election campaign is by helping to advertise the candidate. This is done by handing out leaflets and putting up posters in the constituency. This helps the voting public find out information about the candidate. With this information the voter can discover which candidate will work best to help them. For example, a leaflet may tell an elderly person what the candidate will do to help increase pensions.

continued

continued

A second way in which a supporter can help is by canvassing the electorate. This is when they go round people's doors or telephone their homes, on behalf of the candidate, in order to find out the electorate's thoughts. This is a good way of gaining information, as it will allow the candidate to know if they are meeting the electorate's wishes. For example, if a supporter canvasses families with school age children, they can report back to the candidate on what issues, such as education, are important to families.

Credit question (2006 Q1a)

Candidates rely on help from party workers and volunteers during election campaigns.

Describe, **in detail**, the ways in which party workers and volunteers can help during election campaigns.

(KU, 6 marks)

Look out for

Although the wording is slightly different from the General question, you are being asked the same thing. How can people help during election campaigns?

Look out for

The number of marks awarded to the question. This will let you know how many arguments to give.

Credit answer

An example of **one** paragraph is given below. This is not a complete answer.

There are a number of ways in which party workers and volunteers can help during election campaigns. One such way is through helping to organise meetings in the constituency. They would become involved in this as the candidate would be too busy campaigning and would not be able to afford the time to set up the meeting. Issues such as a venue, publicity for the meeting and organising seating all take time. This is when party workers and volunteers help. An example of this could be if Des McNulty, Labour Party candidate for Clydebank and Milngavie, wished to hold a campaign meeting in Clydebank Town Hall where constituents could come and ask him questions and hear his ideas if he was to become the elected MSP. Mr McNulty would have party workers and volunteers who would carry out all the work to ensure this meeting could take place. As this is an important aspect of campaigning it is vital that candidates have people who can help organise these events, making it an important way workers can help in an election campaign.

For this question, there is only one example answer paragraph provided. By now you should have the understanding and confidence to try and answer the rest of the question yourself.

This paragraph is a detailed, correctly structured answer, which would gain 3 marks. HOWEVER, that is up to the judgement of the marker. In order to aim for full marks for this question, you should imagine that the paragraph will gain you just 2 marks. Therefore you should produce another two arguments, based on the same structure.

Try to complete the answer yourself. Remember to PEER:
POINT = Provide a way party workers and volunteers can help during an election campaign.
EXPLAIN = Explain what this way is and how it helps the campaign.
EXAMPLE = Give an example of the way they are helping.
RELATE = Show how the explanation and example prove that the original point is a way of helping.

Chapter 4 Living in a Democracy

Ways MPs and MSPs represent constituents

What you should know…

> The concept being assessed is **representation**.
> *Ways in which people can act on behalf of others.*

An area you can be questioned on at General and Credit KU levels is 'ways in which MPs and MSPs can represent constituents'.

We have provided below a recap summary to remind you of the main ways. Afterwards there are example General and Credit KU questions and sample answers.

Summary

Remember, there are two areas in which MPs and MSPs can represent you: inside Parliament and in the constituency.

Inside Parliament

- Representatives can ask a Parliamentary question on behalf of constituents. MSPs can do this during First Minister's Question Time and during Ministers' questions. MPs can ask these questions during Prime Minister's Question Time or Ministers' questions. (Look at www.number10.gov.uk.)

- They can take part in and start debates about an issue that affects constituents, such as nuclear bases in their area.

- They can introduce a member's bill in Parliament. This is done on behalf of the best interests of constituents. For example, a member's bill was introduced by Dennis Canavan in 2005 to introduce a St Andrew's Day bank holiday in Scotland to celebrate Scotland and its people. This bill became law in January 2007. For MPs it is known as a Private Member's Bill.

- They can vote on proposed bills in Parliament. This vote will decide whether or not the bill passes to the next stage and ultimately becomes law. An example of this is the bill on tobacco and primary medical services in Scotland, proposed by Nicola Sturgeon MSP in February 2009, to ban tobacco products being displayed and/or advertised. This is currently being discussed and voted upon. (Look at www.scottishparliament.uk.)

- Representatives sit as members of committees. They monitor and question ministers about the work of their departments. For example, your MP may be a member of the work and pensions committee. They will study the work this department does and question the minister in charge of the department, Yvette Cooper MP, about its work and decisions made.

- Any other valid point. (Be aware that this is not a complete list. You may think of other possible ideas and examples yourself.)

continued

Alex Salmond, First Minister of Scotland

The Scottish Parliament chamber

What you should know – continued

In the constituency

- They can attend meetings and events. Your MP/MSP will attend meetings relevant to the constituency, such as a meeting to discuss a mobile phone mast being erected in the constituency. Representatives will also attend events such as the official openings of new buildings.
- Representatives will visit people, write letters and send e-mails. This is in order to respond to the needs of their constituents.
- They will conduct media interviews to draw attention to an issue. For example, Jackie Baillie, MSP for Dumbarton, did a number of television interviews about the C. Diff. bug which killed patients in Vale of Leven Hospital.
- Representatives will contact officials from local councils and Government departments to find out information on behalf of constituents, such as asking the relevant department about the dangers of a nuclear power station in the constituency.
- MPs and MSPs will hold surgeries where constituents can meet with their representative to discuss an issue affecting them. For example, a constituent in Govan could contact their MSP, Nicola Sturgeon, to discuss an issue regarding their local hospital, the Southern General Hospital. (Look at www.writetothem.com.)
- Any other valid point. (Be aware that this is not a complete list. You may think of other possible ideas and examples yourself.)

General questions

There are various wordings for a 'representative' question at General level.

Some examples are:

> Describe **two** ways in which MSPs can represent their constituents. (General 2003 Q1a, 4 marks)

> Describe **one** way in which MSPs find out about problems in their local area.
>
> **AND**
>
> Describe **one** thing the MSP could do to draw attention to problems in his/her local area. (General 2004 Q1c, 4 marks)

> Choose **ONE** of the following representatives.
> - Local councillors
> - MSPs
>
> Describe **two** ways in which the representative you have chosen works on behalf of people in their area. (General 2006 Q1d, 4 marks)

Although these three questions are worded differently, they are asking the **same** thing: 'Ways in which representatives work on behalf of their constituents'.

We will now try an example answer to one of the above questions.

!**Look out for**

Remember to identify the concept before you begin your answer.

!**Look out for**

Take great care when reading the question. Ensure you know **which representative** it asks about and **where** they work. Is it constituency or Parliament?

Chapter 4 Living in a Democracy

General question (2003 Q1a)

> Members of the Scottish Parliament (MSPs) can **represent** their constituents in a number of ways.

Describe **two** ways in which MSPs can **represent** their constituents.

(KU, 4 marks)

General answer

One way in which MSPs can represent their constituents is by asking a question on their behalf, at question time, in Parliament. This is when the MSP, who will already have spoken with the constituent asks a question about an issue that is of concern to the constituency member. For example, if a constituent in the Aberdeen North constituency has a problem concerning hospital treatment in their area, they may speak to their MSP, Brian Adam, who may ask a question to the Health Minister, Nicola Sturgeon.

A second way in which MSPs can represent their constituents is by using the media to put forward issues that are of concern to their constituents. This means they will speak to newspapers, radio or television programmes and use their position to gain publicity for the issue. For example Nigel Don, Scottish National Party MSP for North East Scotland, may use the media to highlight the impact fishing laws have on some of his constituents, who are employed in this industry.

Now you try to answer the other two General questions detailed previously. Remember, the concept is the same.

Credit questions

As at General level, there are various wordings for a 'representative' question at Credit level.

Some examples are:

> Describe, **in detail**, the ways in which MSPs **represent** their constituents in the Scottish Parliament. (Credit 2002 Q1a, 6 marks)

*The key words in this question which separate it from the General question (2003 Q1a) are **in the Scottish Parliament**. This means you must base your answer on what MSPs do in the Parliament.*

> Choose **either** Local Councillors or MSPs or MPs.
>
> Describe, **in detail**, the ways in which the type of representative you have chosen works on behalf of the people they represent. (Credit 2005 Q1a, 6 marks)

The only difference between this question and General (2006 Q1d, 4 marks) is that the Credit has added MPs as a choice for you and it is worth 6 marks. Other than that the question IS exactly the same!

We will now try an example answer to one of the questions.

Credit question (2002 Q1a)

> MSPs represent their constituents in the Scottish Parliament.
>
> Describe, **in detail**, the ways in which MSPs **represent** their constituents in the Scottish Parliament.
>
> (KU, 6 marks)

Annabel Goldie, leader of the Scottish Conservatives

Credit answer

One way MSPs represent their constituents in the Scottish Parliament is by asking a Parliamentary question. This means a constituency or regional MSP can ask a question either to the First Minister at First Minister's Question Time or to department ministers about an issue affecting their constituents. They do this to get a response they can take back to the constituency or region they represent. For example, Annabel Goldie, a regional MSP for West of Scotland, may ask First Minister, Alex Salmond, a question about the cost of staging the Commonwealth Games in Glasgow in 2014. This will have an impact on the residents of this region, as money will have to pay for the games. Therefore asking a Parliamentary question is a major way of representing constituents, as it aims to gain information which can have an impact on them.

A further way is by contacting a minister who is in charge of a particular area. An MSP will speak to or e-mail a minister to find out the answer to an issue a constituent has. For example, if a constituent in the Govan area of Glasgow has been wrongly convicted of a crime, they may contact their constituency MSP, Nicola Sturgeon, who could then contact the Cabinet Secretary for Justice, Kenny MacAskill MSP, in order to gain information to establish what their position is regarding the conviction. This shows that being able to contact a cabinet minister is important as it is a way for a constituent to gain information regarding an important issue.

A final way is by introducing a member's bill. This is when an MSP will put forward an issue that they think is important enough to become a law for the country and its people. They will introduce it in Parliament. If a majority of MSPs vote in favour of the bill it becomes law. For example, Hugh Henry, MSP for Paisley South, introduced a member's bill in June 2009, to make it a specific criminal offence to attack a worker, such as a train ticket collector, who has face to face contact with the public. This is a way for Mr Henry to represent both his constituents and other people in the country. Therefore introducing a member's bill is a way of representing constituents as these bills become laws which help protect them.

This paragraph is a detailed, correctly structured answer, which should gain 3 marks. **HOWEVER** that is up to the judgement of the marker. In order to gain full marks for this question, you should imagine that the paragraph will gain you just 2 marks. Therefore you should produce another two arguments, based on the same structure.

Chapter 4 Living in a Democracy

The previous answer should gain the full 6 marks. The detail of your answer may be different. However the structure should be the same throughout.

- Read the question carefully, understanding what you are being asked, the number of marks and the concept.
- Give your argument.
- Explain the argument.
- Give an example to back up the argument and explanation.
- Provide a relationship, showing how the example highlights the point as an argument.

Your content can be different. You can have a different PEER. BUT, if you use this method correctly, you should gain the same number of marks as the answer given on the previous page.

Rights of citizens when opposing new laws

What you should know…

> The concept being assessed is **rights**. *The rights people have when they disagree with decisions.*

An area you can be questioned on at Credit KU level is 'Describe, **in detail**, the rights that people have when opposing the introduction of new laws'. To date this has not been questioned at General level.

We have provided below a recap summary to remind you of the main ways. Afterwards there is an example Credit KU question and sample answer.

Summary

- People can demonstrate and protest about issues and laws outside Government and public buildings in order to get their point across.
- People can use the media to draw attention to the issue. This gives the opportunity to get the point across to a wider audience.
- People can lobby their MP/MSP. People can visit the various Parliaments and speak to their representatives. One of the founding principles of the Scottish Parliament is access and participation, meaning it is there for the people.
- People can send letters and e-mails to representatives and ministers to give their views on issues.
- People have the right to set up petitions in the community and online to allow people to register their support and opinions regarding issues.
- Any other valid point. (Be aware that this is not a complete list. You may think of other possible ideas and examples yourself.)

! Look out for

This area has not previously been examined at General level. **HOWEVER**, this does not mean it will not be asked at some time in the future.

Standard Grade Modern Studies

Credit question (2007 Q1a)

Describe, **in detail**, the rights that people have when opposing the introduction of new laws.

(KU, 4 marks)

> **Look out for**
>
> Pay close attention to key words in the question: **rights, opposing, new laws**.

Credit answer

An example of **one** paragraph is given below. This is not a complete answer.

> There are a number of rights people have when opposing the introduction of new laws. One right is being able to protest and demonstrate outside Government buildings. This is when those people opposed to the law gather with banners and a firm message of opposition towards the Government. This can have a positive impact as it brings pressure to the Government from people who are also voters and it can bring media attention. An example of this was when young people recently protested outside the Scottish Parliament to show their unhappiness at Scottish Government plans to raise the legal age for buying alcohol from 18 to 21 years. Some young people felt it was an unfair penalty on those who drink responsibly. Because of this the Government have decided to further investigate the issue. This shows that demonstrating and protesting is a good way of opposing decisions as it can encourage Governments to reconsider their plans if they know there is voter disagreement.

Use the recap summary for this question to try to provide a second argument for this answer.

Reasons why specific groups are under-represented

What you should know…

> The concept being assessed is **representation**. *Ways in which people can have their say on issues.*

An area you can be questioned on at Credit level is 'Reasons why women and/or ethnic minorities are under-represented in Parliament'. This can make reference to **both** the United Kingdom and Scottish Parliaments. To date this has not been questioned at General level.

We have provided below a recap summary to remind you of the main ways. Afterwards there is an example Credit KU question and sample answer.

continued

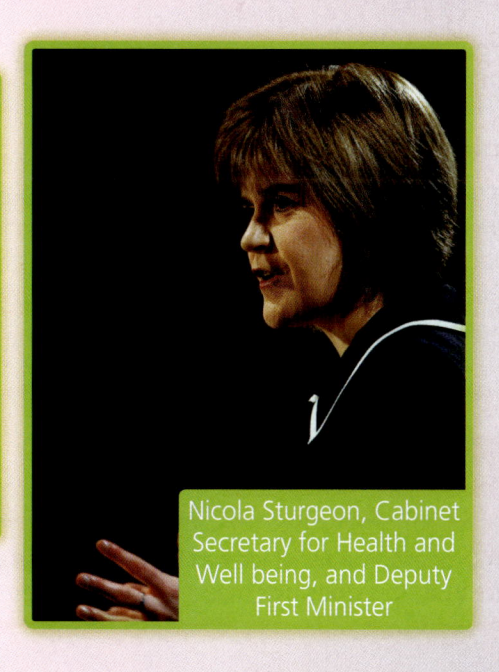

Nicola Sturgeon, Cabinet Secretary for Health and Well being, and Deputy First Minister

Chapter 4 Living in a Democracy

What you should know – continued

Summary

Women

- Politics has traditionally been a male dominated environment. This can lead to women lacking confidence and feeling intimidated.
- Constituencies may feel reluctant to choose women as candidates as it may go against the history of candidates in the area. Therefore a woman may be less likely to win.
- Women are often under-represented due to family commitments. Women are the main child carers. This makes it harder to work away from home, such as in the House of Commons in London.
- Until recently the House of Commons still had male clubs. This may make the atmosphere very intimidating for women.
- Parliamentary debates usually have a confrontational style. Many women do not like this style. They prefer a consensus, calm approach. The style of debating may put them off entering politics.
- If women have time off to have children, this can make it harder to break into politics in later life.
- Any other valid point. (Be aware that this is not a complete list. You may think of other possible ideas and examples yourself.)

HOWEVER!

The Scottish Parliament has brought about a change in female representation in politics.

- A major aim of the Scottish Parliament was to get more people involved in its work and decisions.
- The working hours of the Parliament are much more 'family friendly'. They are normal 9am–5pm hours, as opposed to London, where work can go on late into the evening.
- Parliament holidays tend to follow Scottish school holidays, meaning MSPs can spend time with their families.
- The Parliament has crèche facilities for MSPs to bring their young children, where they know they will be looked after. The Westminster Parliament does not have this facility.
- The AMS voting system used has helped more women be voted in due to its wider regional representation.
- Any other valid point. (Be aware that this is not a complete list. You may think of other possible ideas and examples yourself.)

Ethnic minorities

- Prejudice and racism still exist in society and in politics. This is evident in the growing popularity of extreme political parties. The selection process for candidates reflects this. Some parties may not select a candidate if they think the electorate will not vote for them.
- Both the Westminster and Scottish Parliaments are still mainly white male environments. The Scottish Parliament has no ethnic minority MSPs at the moment.

continued

Look out for!

This is a question area which has **NEVER** been examined at General level.
HOWEVER, this **does not** mean it will not be examined at some stage in the future.

What you should know – continued

- Levels of education are traditionally lower for black Britons. There is a close link between education and politics, making it harder for such groups to break through.
- There is a real lack of ethnic minority role models to look up to. If you cannot identify someone who has already achieved, then you are less likely to be encouraged to go for it yourself. Ethnic minority groups make up 8% of the British population, but make up only 2·3% (15 out of 646) of MPs after the 2005 General Election.
- Any other valid point. (Be aware that this is not a complete list. You may think of other possible ideas and examples yourself.)

!Look out for

This area has been examined **twice** before at Credit level. It could appear again!

Credit questions

Choose either women or ethnic minorities.

Explain, **in detail**, why the group you have chosen is **under-represented** in the House of Commons. (2003 Q1a, 4 marks)

Explain, in detail, the reasons why women are better represented in the Scottish Parliament than at Westminster. (2008 Q1b, 4 marks)

By now you should have a good grasp of how the process works for answering a Credit KU question. Use the PEER technique and the summary above to try to answer the two questions yourself.

REMEMBER! You must include relevant examples in your answer.

Advantages and disadvantages of voting systems

What you should know…

> The concept being assessed is **representation**. *Ways in which people can have their say on issues.*

An area you can be questioned on at Credit level is 'voting systems'. You can be asked to describe the advantages of various systems.

We have provided below a recap summary to remind you of the main advantages. Afterwards there is an example Credit KU question and sample answer. To date this question has not been examined at General level. **HOWEVER**, this **does not** mean it will not be examined at some stage in the future!

continued

Chapter 4 Living in a Democracy

What you should know – continued

Summary

At Credit level, teaching will focus on First Past the Post (FPTP), the Additional Member System (AMS) and Single Transferable Vote (STV). These systems will be examined as long as they are still used in Scotland/UK. Candidates will always be given a choice of voting system to answer on.

FPTP

Advantages

- It is thought to be fair, as the candidate with more votes than any other candidate in the constituency wins.
- It is simple and easy to understand. It delivers a quick result, as voters simply place an X next to the candidate's name.
- It usually will provide a clear national winner. This lessens the chance of a coalition government.
- FPTP gives a stronger personal link between the constituency and the representative.
- Any other valid point. (Be aware that this is not a complete list. You may think of other possible ideas and examples yourself.)

AMS

Advantages

- The number of representatives each party gains is more in line with the percentage of votes cast for the party. Therefore it better reflects the wishes of the people.
- AMS gives a greater incentive to vote as fewer votes are wasted. This will encourage people to vote.
- It gives smaller parties a chance to gain seats as, for example in Scotland, they succeed in the second regional vote. It has helped the Green Party to gain MSPs.
- AMS means that if a party does not get a majority of the votes, they will not become the Government. This better reflects the wishes of the people. If more people do not vote for a party than vote for them, why should they form the Government? AMS stops this from happening.
- Any other valid point. (Be aware that this is not a complete list. You may think of other possible ideas and examples yourself.)

STV

Advantages

- STV gives smaller parties a better chance of being elected. It breaks the big party domination.
- There are no wasted votes. Votes get relocated to a voter's next choice.
- STV encourages parties to work together, as coalitions are much more likely to happen. It also reflects the way people voted.
- Any other valid point. (Be aware that this is not a complete list. You may think of other possible ideas and examples yourself.)

Credit question (2007 Q1b)

Choose **one** of the following electoral systems.

A. Single Transferable Vote
B. Additional Member System
C. First Past the Post

Explain, **in detail**, the **advantages** of the electoral system you have chosen.

(KU, 6 marks)

*This is a straightforward question. It simply asks you for advantages. **Nothing else**. Make sure you know the advantages of at least one of the systems well. You still must PEER in this answer. Remember to give examples.*

Credit answer

An example of **one** paragraph is given below. This is not a complete answer.

There are a number of advantages to First Past the Post, which is the system used to elect representatives to the UK Parliament. One advantage of FPTP is that it is a simple fast system to use and easy for voters to understand. Voters simply place a cross in the box next to the candidate they wish to vote for. Once they have done this they place it in the ballot box. There is no complicated ranking of candidates, as with other systems. Because of this simple cross, votes can be counted quickly and a result can be known within hours. For example, voters in the East Dunbartonshire constituency who voted for Jo Swinson as their MP simply placed an X next to her name and within hours they knew their vote had helped her win the seat. Therefore because of this system being simple to use and understand it helps encourage people to go out and vote.

Try to complete the rest of the answer for the full 6 marks.

Chapter 4 Living in a Democracy

Trade unions

What you should know…

There are five areas you can be questioned on at General and/or Credit level regarding trade unions in Living in a Democracy:

- Ways members can participate in trade unions.
- Actions union members can take to support their union during a dispute.
- Rights and responsibilities of union members.
- Rights of members during a dispute.
- Problems shop stewards can help with and how they help.

A Scottish shipyard

Look out for

Quite often trade union questions are similar in their wording.

Ways members can participate in trade unions

What you should know…

> The concept being assessed is **participation**.
> *Ways members can take part in activities.*

An area you can be questioned on at General level is 'ways in which members can take part in trade union activities'. So far this area has not been examined at Credit level. **HOWEVER**, it may be examined at some stage.

We have provided below a recap summary to remind you of the main ways. Afterwards there is a sample General question and answer.

Summary

- Members can stand as a candidate for a position, such as a shop steward. This is the person who is the representative of the workers. He/she is the link between the workers and the employer and also between the workers and the union.
- Members can attend union meetings to debate issues and raise their views. At meetings members will hear about the work of the union and the issues of importance. The more members who attend meetings the stronger the union and the fairer the decisions made.
- Members can vote during union elections. They can vote for representatives, such as shop stewards, and they can vote on possible union action, such as going on strike.
- Members can take part in industrial action. If members are threatened with wage cuts or overtime reductions, they may decide to take industrial action in order to change the employer's decision. Types of action could be strikes, picket lines, go-slows, etc.
- Any other valid point. (Be aware that this is not a complete list. You may think of other possible ideas and examples yourself. Look at www.tuc.org.uk.)

Standard Grade Modern Studies

General question (2002 Q1a)

> More members should **take part** in trade union activities.
>
> Describe **two** ways in which members can **take part** in trade union activities.
>
> (KU, 4 marks)

Look out for

Carefully note the wording of the question. The key words are **take part**.

General answer

> There are a number of ways members of a trade union can take part in activities. One way is by standing as a candidate for a position, such as a shop steward. This is when a union member decides to stand for election to become the person who represents the workers in talks with management and who reports member views to the overall union. For example, Jamie Webster stood as a candidate to become the shop steward for Govan shipyard. He represented the workers when the yard was under the threat of job losses.
>
> A second way members can take part in union activities is by taking part in industrial action. This is when members are unhappy at decisions that have been made by employers. In order to get the decision changed workers vote on taking industrial action such as going on strike. An example of this took place in August 2008, when council employees were unhappy at their pay conditions. To try to gain an increase they voted for strike action. This impacted on services as workers such as school janitors and learning assistants went on strike from work for a day. This can force employers into rethinking their decisions, so these interruptions do not happen again.

Remember: Point, Explain, Example!

Actions union members can take during a dispute

What you should know…

> The concept being assessed is **participation**.
> Ways members can take part.

An area you can be questioned on at General level is 'actions union members can take to support their union during a dispute'. So far this area has not been examined at Credit level. **HOWEVER** this **does not** mean it will not be examined at some stage in the future.

We have provided below a recap summary to remind you of the main points. Afterwards there is a sample General question and answer.

A picket line

continued

29

Chapter 4 Living in a Democracy

What you should know – continued

Summary

- Union members can vote for a range of industrial actions. This shows support, as the more members who vote, the fairer the decision, as it represents the view of more workers.
- Members can carry out industrial action, such as going on strike.
- Members can support by providing evidence of any problems at work, such as unsafe working conditions.
- Members can attend marches and demonstrations against employers. The greater the support, the more seriously the union will be taken.
- Members can speak to the media to highlight issues of concern, such as closure threats.
- Any other valid point. (Be aware that this is not a complete list. You may think of other possible ideas and examples yourself. Look at www.unison.org.uk.)

General question (2004 Q1a)

> Trade union members can support their union during a dispute.

Describe **two** actions which trade union members can take to support their union during a dispute.

(KU, 4 marks)

Look out for

Always know how many reasons the question is asking for and give this exact number of reasons.

General answer

An example of **one** paragraph is given below. This is not a complete answer.

> One action which trade union members can take to support their union during a dispute is voting for industrial action. This is when union members attend a meeting, hear the issue and the possible ways industrial action can solve the issue. They then vote in secret. It is important they attend and vote, as if there are 200 members in the workplace and only 50 of them attend, this is not showing support or representing the view of most of the workers. For example, during the fire fighters' dispute over pay, it was important they all voted for industrial action, as their strike could have a direct impact on lives.

> Using the summary and having read the sample answer for the first action, try to complete a paragraph answer for the second action. Remember to PEE! (Ask your teacher to mark the paragraph for you.)

Rights and responsibilities of union members

What you should know…

> The concept being assessed is **rights and responsibilities**.
> *To exercise the freedoms and choices we have.*

An area you can be questioned on at both General and Credit levels in varying ways is 'the rights and responsibilities that trade union members have'.

We have provided below a recap summary to remind you of the main points. Afterwards there are sample General and Credit questions and answers.

Summary

- Members have the right to take industrial action, such as going on strike and forming picket lines. The responsibility is to stay within the law and not to intimidate people or damage property. Also, all workers must support action taken.
- Members have the right to attend union meetings and voice their opinion. The responsibility is to listen to other views and accept decisions that are made.
- Members also have the right to vote for elected representatives, such as shop stewards. The responsibility is to vote in a correct fashion and accept the candidate with the most votes.
- Members have the right to be consulted on decisions and informed of their progress. The responsibility is they then support decisions.
- Members have the right to be represented by their shop steward. The responsibility is to accept their advice on an issue.
- Any other valid point. (Be aware that this is not a complete list. You may think of other possible ideas and examples yourself. Look at www.news.bbc.co.uk.)

General question (2006 Q1a)

> Trade union members have rights and responsibilities.
>
> Describe **one** right and **one** responsibility that a trade union member has.
>
> (KU, 4 marks)

Remember: 1 right and 1 responsibility!

Chapter 4 Living in a Democracy

General answer

One right that a trade union member has is the right to take industrial action. This is when a member, along with other union members, votes to take action such as striking from work. Members do this if they are unhappy about conditions of their work. For example, in early 2009, workers in the oil refinery sector voted to strike after jobs were given to foreign workers from European Union countries who worked for less money, rather than to British workers.

The responsibility that accompanies industrial action, though, is to ensure that it does not break the law. Workers who strike or form picket lines cannot be violent or cause criminal damage. This meant that the oil workers who demonstrated had to do so peacefully. They couldn't, for example, commit criminal acts against the foreign workers when they were arriving at work.

Look out for

The difference between the General and Credit questions.

Credit question (2003 Q1b)

Trade union members have rights and responsibilities during a dispute with their employees.

Describe, **in detail**, the **rights and responsibilities** trade union members have during a dispute with their employers.

(KU, 6 marks)

Can you spot the key difference between this Credit question and the General question above? Both questions ask about rights and responsibilities, BUT the Credit question focuses on them during a dispute with employers. This means you can only answer on this area and you **can't** include some of the suggestions in the summary, such as the right to vote for a candidate and attending union meetings. If you did, you would not be answering the Credit question as these suggestions **DO NOT** deal with disputes with an employer. Try to answer this question yourself.

Rights of members during disputes

Credit question (2008 Q1a)

Trade union members have **rights during a dispute** with their employers.

Describe, **in detail**, the **rights** trade union members have **during a dispute** with their employers.

(KU, 4 marks)

There is one key difference between this question and the previous question from 2003. This one examines **only rights**. You do not answer on responsibilities.

Credit answer

An example of **one** paragraph is given below. This is not a complete answer.

> Trade union members have many rights during a dispute with their employers. One right they have is to receive representation from a union official, such as a shop steward, during the dispute. This is when the employee will consult the advice of the shop steward if they have a problem, such as holiday entitlement. The shop steward will speak to the employer in order to try and reach a settlement to the dispute. For example, if an employee of a supermarket had a request for holidays accepted, booked a holiday and then had their time off changed by their employer, they would consult their shop steward, who would speak to management about the issue, in order to try to reach a solution. As the shop steward is trained in all contractual matters they are in a position to negotiate with the employer to reach a satisfactory agreement for the union member.

Use the PEER method to complete the second part of this 4 mark answer.

Problems shop stewards help with and how they help

What you should know…

> The concept being assessed is **representation**.
> *Ways in which people can act on behalf of others.*

An area you can be questioned on at General level is 'the problems shop stewards can help union members with and the ways they can help'.

We have provided below a recap summary to remind you of the main ways. Afterwards there is a sample General question.

This question type has not been examined to date at Credit level. **However**, this **does not** mean it will not be examined at some stage in the future.

Summary

Problems

- Members may be told they will not receive a wage increase this year. With the current 'credit crunch' this is a problem which will affect a lot of employees.
- Members may have health and safety concerns over their working conditions. Employers may not be investing in correct safety equipment.
- A lack of training courses for workers may be a problem. Workers might feel they do not have the correct skills for the jobs they are doing.
- Any other valid point. (Be aware that this is not a complete list. You may think of other possible ideas and examples yourself. Look at www.tuc.org.uk.)

continued

Chapter 4 Living in a Democracy

What you should know – continued

Shop steward help

- Shop stewards can arrange meetings and talk to the management to reach an agreement over things such as wage increases.
- Stewards can call meetings with all members and arrange ballots on industrial action.
- They can coordinate industrial action, such as work to rule and strike action.
- They can try to arrange correct training courses for workers.
- Any other valid point. (Be aware that this is not a complete list. You may think of other possible ideas and examples yourself.)

General question (2007 Q1c)

> Shop stewards help union members in a number of different ways.

Give **two** problems that a shop steward might help their members with.

For **one** of these problems, describe how the shop steward might help.

(KU, 4 marks)

Use the PEE method and the summary to answer this question yourself.

Look out for!

Notice the number of things the question is asking you: **two** problems, but only **one** way of helping.

Pressure groups

What you should know…

There are three areas you can be questioned on at General and Credit levels regarding pressure groups in Living in a Democracy:

- Actions pressure groups can take to influence Government decisions.
- Rights and responsibilities of pressure group members.
- Rights and responsibilities of specific pressure groups.

GREENPEACE
www.greenpeace.org.uk

Look out for!

Quite often pressure group questions are similar in their wording.

Standard Grade Modern Studies

Pressure group actions

What you should know…

> The concept being assessed is **participation**. *Ways pressure groups can take part in decision making.*

An area you can be questioned on at General level is 'actions pressure groups can take to try to influence the Government'.

This question type has not been examined to date at Credit level. **HOWEVER**, this **does not** mean it will not be examined at some stage in the future.

We have provided below a recap summary to remind you of the main ways. Afterwards there is a sample General question and answer.

Summary

- Groups can send leaflets and letters to people in a local area to make them aware of a decision which may affect them.
- Groups can use the media and celebrities to increase public awareness of an issue. The more support for an issue, the more pressure is put on the Government.
- Groups can use petition campaigns, where people sign their name supporting the group or disagreeing with the decision.
- Groups can hold demonstrations/marches to help highlight their disagreement with the decision.
- Groups can contact a representative from the Government to speak to them and put forward the group's views.
- Groups can lobby MPs to try to convince them to support the group's views.
- Groups can collect statistics and evidence to use in the media.
- Any other valid point. (Be aware that this is not a complete list. You may think of other possible ideas and examples yourself. Look at www.greenpeace.org.uk.)

Now try to complete the following question. Make sure you use relevant examples.

General question (2005 Q1a)

> Pressure groups can take different actions to try to influence the Government.

Describe **two** actions which pressure groups can take to try to influence the Government.

(KU, 4 marks)

Look out for

The wording of the question: **influence the Government**.

Chapter 4 Living in a Democracy

General answer

An example of **one** paragraph is given below. This is not a complete answer.

> One action pressure groups can take is to use the media and celebrities in their campaigns. *This is a method they use to influence the ideas of larger numbers of people. They use the media to get the information to people in the country. If these people agree it adds to the numbers putting pressure on the Government.* For example, the Gurkha population in Britain who were refused the right to stay in the country, used the media and the celebrity Joanna Lumley to help change the decision of the Government. This pressure helped persuade the Government to change its mind.

Look out for

You can contact organisations to find out what work they do. For example, you might contact Greenpeace to ask questions or get information about the work they do. The websites of the organisation will usually have contact details.

Try to provide the second action to complete this answer.

Rights and responsibilities of pressure groups and their members

What you should know…

> The concept being assessed is **rights and responsibilities**.
> *To exercise the freedoms and choices we have.*

An area you can be questioned on at both General and Credit levels is 'the rights and responsibilities of pressure groups and their members'.

We have provided below a recap summary to remind you of the main issues. Afterwards there are sample General and Credit questions and answers.

One thing you should remember is that rights of pressure groups and actions are the same. Groups have the right to petition. An action groups can take is to petition.

Protestors being arrested

Summary

- Groups have the right to hold a protest march or demonstration in a public place, such as a city centre. Supporters are allowed to carry banners and voice opinions to publicise their cause. The responsibility is to ensure they do this peacefully, within the law and do not hurt or damage.

- Groups have the right to use the media to attract attention to their cause. They often use publicity stunts to highlight their point. The responsibility is to ensure they are truthful to the media and their publicity does not cause harm. They also cannot slander or libel people through the media.

A demonstration in Westminster

continued

Standard Grade Modern Studies

What you should know – continued

- Groups can organise petitions which supporters sign to show the level of support for their cause. These petitions are then given to the organisation the group is trying to influence. The responsibility is to make sure the signatures are genuine.
- Any other valid point. (Be aware that this is not a complete list. You may think of other possible ideas and examples yourself. Look at www.wwf.org.uk and www.countrysidealliance.org.)

General question (2008 Q1a)

> Members of pressure groups have rights and responsibilities.
>
> Describe one **right** and one **responsibility** that members of a pressure group have.
>
> (KU, 4 marks)

*You **must be aware** that this question asks for **one right** and **one responsibility**.*

General answer

> One right that pressure groups have is the right to protest and demonstrate. This is when a group publicises its cause to the decision makers by staging a demonstration in a busy public area to get their point across. For example, the 'Stop the War Coalition' demonstration in London, where it is thought a million people marched from Piccadilly Circus to Hyde Park to demonstrate against the war in Iraq, trying to influence the Government's decision to send soldiers to Iraq.
>
> With rights come responsibilities. One responsibility is to act within the law. This is when pressure groups carry out their right in a responsible and lawful way. For example the 'Stop the War Coalition' had the responsibility to ensure that a million people marching and demonstrating through London on a Saturday afternoon did so peacefully, without breaking the law or causing damage to property.

Credit question (2004 Q1a)

The following Credit question about rights and responsibilities of pressure groups and their members takes a slightly more detailed approach than the General question we have just looked at.

The General question asked for one right and one responsibility of members. The Credit question is a little more complex.

> Pressure groups in the UK have **rights and responsibilities** in any actions they take in trying to influence public opinion and Government policy.
>
> Describe, **in detail**, the **rights and responsibilities** of pressure groups.
>
> (KU, 8 marks)

Chapter 4 Living in a Democracy

This Credit question has slight differences in the wording and the way you would answer it. The General question asked about pressure group **members**. The Credit question focuses specifically on **pressure groups**. In reality the rights and responsibilities of both categories are the same. The major difference is that in the Credit question you **must** refer to the pressure group throughout. Therefore you need to have knowledge about pressure groups and examples of issues they are involved with. This will allow you to provide details of rights and responsibilities with regards to these issues.

When answering a Credit question that asks you to focus on two issues (rights **AND** responsibilities) you can complete your answer in one of two ways. Either match each right you decide to use with its responsibility **OR** answer about a number of rights **followed** by a number of responsibilities. Possibly the first approach is the easiest way to answer the question.

Study the example answer below. We will complete the first paragraph together, then you try to complete the rest of the answer.

Credit answer

An example of **one** paragraph is given below. This is not a complete answer.

One right a pressure group has is the right to use the media to publicise their cause to try to change decisions. They use media such as newspapers to inform the public of the issue they are campaigning to change. This informs more people, who the group hope will add their support to the issue. This is a method they use, as the decision maker is more likely to listen to opinions of a larger number of people. For example, Greenpeace was involved in a campaign to stop disused oil rigs being dumped at sea. They saw this as being bad for the environment and sea life. To put pressure on Shell Oil and the Government, Greenpeace took out full page newspaper space detailing the plans of the oil company and telling the public why it was a bad thing. They encouraged the public to boycott the use of the oil company's petrol stations. This saw a drop in the amount of money made by Shell. This in the end forced Shell to drop their plan to dump rigs at sea. Therefore this shows how important the right to use media campaigns can be as it is a major way of informing large numbers of the public.

With this right, however, comes a responsibility. Pressure groups must ensure they are truthful and give correct information when using the media in their campaign. This means that they must research all the facts and make sure that the information they give to the media is correct and does not tell any lies about the decision they are trying to change. For example, during the campaign against Shell, Greenpeace had to make sure that their news articles about the amount of oil and pollution which would affect the sea, contained the correct information and figures. They couldn't say that 500 litres of oil would leak into the sea if the actual figure was 10 litres. Therefore it is important that pressure groups are responsible when using the media as incorrect information can damage the company whose decision they are trying to change and it can also affect their own reputation.

Changing Society — Chapter 5

The elderly

What you should know…

There are four key areas you can be questioned on at General and/or Credit levels regarding the elderly in Changing Society.

- The types of housing available to the elderly and how it meets their needs.
- The reasons why the health needs of some elderly people are greater than others.
- Wealth differences between sections of the elderly.
- The ways in which the needs of the elderly can be met.

! Look out for

The area being examined in the question. Questions about the ways the needs of the elderly can be met, for example, may be worded in various ways.

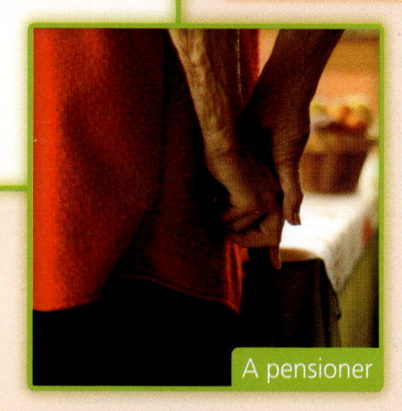

A pensioner

The types of housing available to the elderly

What you should know…

The concept being assessed is **need**. How does housing meet needs?

An area you can be questioned on at General and Credit Knowledge and Understanding (KU) levels is 'the ways different types of housing help meet the needs of elderly people'.

Below is a summary recap to help remind you of some of the main points of this area. Following that there are a number of KU General and Credit questions that you could be asked about. They have some differences in their wording, but they focus on the same area, i.e. housing meeting the needs of the elderly. There are sample answers to go with them.

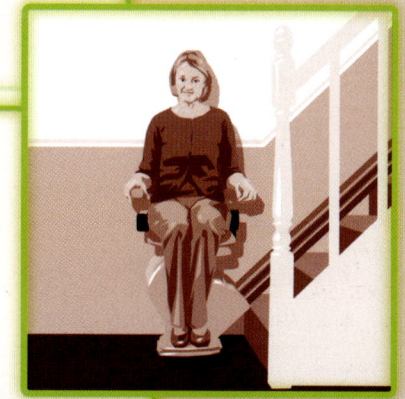

Summary
Adapted homes

An elderly person's current home can be adapted to meet their needs in a number of ways:

- Stair lifts can be installed to take an elderly person up and down stairs to the bathroom, kitchen, etc. This can be a huge help if the person has hip or balance problems and difficulty using the stairs.

continued

39

Chapter 5 Changing Society

What you should know – continued

- Lever taps may be installed to aid the process of turning taps on and off. This is particularly helpful if the person is suffering from arthritis in the hands.
- Ramps can be installed to allow access to the house. If the house originally had steps to climb to the entrance this may now prove difficult for an elderly person. Ramps would help overcome this problem.
- Walk-in appliances such as baths can be installed. This allows the elderly person to open a door and walk into the bath. This helps if they have joint or muscle problems.
- Any other valid point. (Be aware that this is not a complete list. You may think of other possible ideas and examples yourself. Look at www.helptheaged.org.uk.)

Community care

Community care, provided within a person's own home, can help meet needs in a number of ways:

- Adaptations, such as stair lifts, can help movement and allow elderly people to remain in their own homes.
- Intercoms are fitted to homes by community care to provide security for residents.
- Personal care plans can be drawn up to provide medical care, such as visits from nurses and GPs to tend to wounds and give prescriptions.
- Community care provides a meals on wheels service where meals are provided to the elderly person in their own home. This helps ensure they get the correct dietary requirements.
- Community care helps the person remain happy and content, as they are in their own home with familiar surroundings and possessions.
- Any other valid point. (Be aware that this is not a complete list. You may think of other possible ideas and examples yourself.)

Sheltered housing

Sheltered housing can help meet an elderly person's needs in a number of ways:

- In sheltered housing all rooms are on the same level. This means there are no issues with stairs.
- Sheltered housing has all necessary facilities such as plug sockets and light fittings at easy to reach points. This means an elderly person will not have to bend down to plug sockets.
- There is a sense of security that a person may not get in their own house. They are living in a security controlled complex with other people and there is a warden on call 24/7 to help with any problems. This helps give a sense of independence but also security.
- There is ramped access to allow wheelchair access to an elderly person's home.
- In sheltered housing there is a communal lounge to allow social activities with other elderly people. This helps develop a social life.
- Any other valid point. (Be aware that this is not a complete list. You may think of other possible ideas and examples yourself.)

A sheltered housing complex

continued

Standard Grade Modern Studies

What you should know – continued

Residential care homes

Residential care housing can help meet an elderly person's needs in a number of ways:

- Residential care tends to be for those elderly people with more complex health problems. Trained nursing staff is employed 24 hours a day in the care home to care for those with physical needs, such as stroke victims, and to provide rehabilitation programmes after operations.
- Residential housing provides specific diets to ensure residents receive the correct nutrients and food groups.
- Residential homes are specially designed with ramps and wider door frames for wheelchair users.
- Any other valid point. (Be aware that this is not a complete list. You may think of other possible ideas and examples yourself.)

Nursing care housing

Nursing care housing can help meet an elderly person's needs in a number of ways:

- Nursing care housing helps care for people with serious health problems, such as dementia or Alzheimer's. Trained nursing staff provide for the care needs of residents 24 hours a day.
- Nursing care staff are trained to control and administer medication to residents.
- Nursing housing provides specific diets to ensure residents receive the correct nutrients and food groups.
- Nursing care can help prolong the life of patients with serious medical conditions.
- Any other valid point. (Be aware that this is not a complete list. You may think of other possible ideas and examples yourself.)

However, some elderly people live in housing that does not meet their needs anymore.

There are many reasons for this:

- If it is a family home, it may now be too big for the person to manage on their own, now their children have left. A family home will be difficult and expensive for them to maintain, especially if they are relying on a pension as their main income.
- If the house needs repairs, the person may not be able to afford these. They may find it very difficult to sell the house without these repairs.
- Due to illness or disability, the housing may be unsuitable, if it has stairs, upstairs bathroom, etc.
- Any other valid point. (Be aware that this is not a complete list. You may think of other possible ideas and examples yourself.)

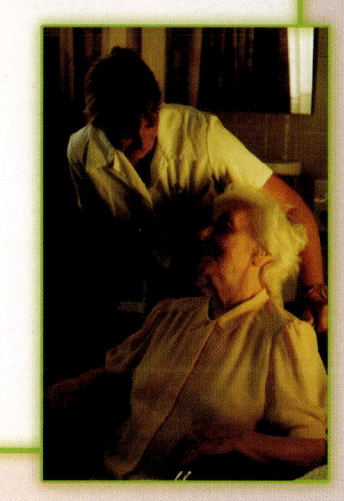

General questions

> Many elderly people live in their own homes. Some of these homes have been adapted to meet their needs.

Give **two ways** in which homes can be adapted to meet the needs of some elderly people.

For **each** way explain how it meets their needs. (2006 Q2a, 4 marks)

Chapter 5 Changing Society

> Sheltered housing can help meet the **needs** of elderly people.

Describe **two** ways in which sheltered housing can help meet the **needs** of elderly people. (2009 Q2a, 4 marks)

To answer this question, you may wish to use the drawing below.

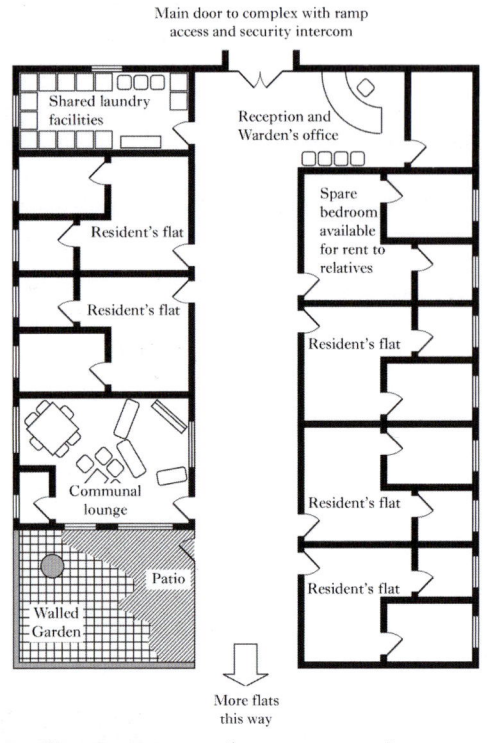

[Floor plan diagram showing sheltered housing complex with: Main door to complex with ramp access and security intercom, Shared laundry facilities, Reception and Warden's office, Spare bedroom available for rent to relatives, Resident's flats, Communal lounge, Walled Garden, Patio, and arrow indicating "More flats this way"]

You must be aware of the different benefits of each type of housing in order to answer these questions.

> We will provide an answer to the 2006 question. The key thing to look out for in this question is the second part: 'For **each** way explain how it meets their needs.' You must answer both parts in order to get full marks.

General answer (2006 Q2a)

An example of **one** paragraph is given below. This is not a complete answer.

> Elderly people can remain in their own homes due to houses being adapted to meet their needs. One way this can be done is through stair lifts being installed. This may happen if the elderly person lives in a house where essential rooms are situated upstairs. The lift will help take them up and down stairs. For example, if the bathroom is situated upstairs the elderly person can use the stair lift to get to it. (2) This meets their needs as it will be much quicker and if the elderly person has hip problems, using stairs could be difficult. A stair lift will solve this and allow the person to remain in their home.

*The number (2) shows you where the second part of the question is answered: 'For **each** way explain how it meets their needs.' You should see how this section of the paragraph answers that point.*

Now try to complete the answer, giving the second way.

Credit questions

> Some elderly people in the UK live in housing that does not meet their **needs**.
>
> Explain, **in detail**, why some older people in the UK live in housing that does not meet their **needs**. (2004 Q2a, 4 marks)

*The two Credit questions related to housing are different. The second asks how a specific type of care meets the needs. However, the first asks why some elderly live in housing that **does not** meet their needs.*

> | Community care within their own home | Sheltered housing | Residential care homes |
>
> Choose **one** type of care from the options above.
>
> Explain, **in detail**, the ways in which this type of care **meets the needs** of some elderly people. (2008 Q2a, 8 marks)

Use the summaries for each type of housing to complete your own answer to each of these questions.

Health needs of the elderly

What you should know…

> The concepts being assessed are **equality and need**.
> *What are the health needs of the elderly?*

An area you can be questioned on at General and Credit levels is 'why some elderly people are healthier than others OR why some elderly have greater health needs than others'.

Below is a recap summary to remind you of the main points of this area. Afterwards there are sample questions and answers.

Although these two possibilities are worded slightly differently they look at the same issue and ask the same question. 'Health needs of some elderly people are different to others, WHY?' The first possibility reflects the wording of a General question, the second possibility reflects the wording of a Credit question.

Summary

- Health problems increase with rising age. Elderly people who are aged 75 and over are at greater risk of illness than a person aged 65.
- There is a prominent link between poverty and ill health. Poorer elderly people face greater health problems, caused by, for example, not being able to afford to heat their homes (which can lead to illness such as hypothermia), or not being able to afford exercise and a good diet of fresh and healthy foods.
- Elderly people who are poorer are more likely to smoke and drink and lack physical exercise. These issues lead to health problems.

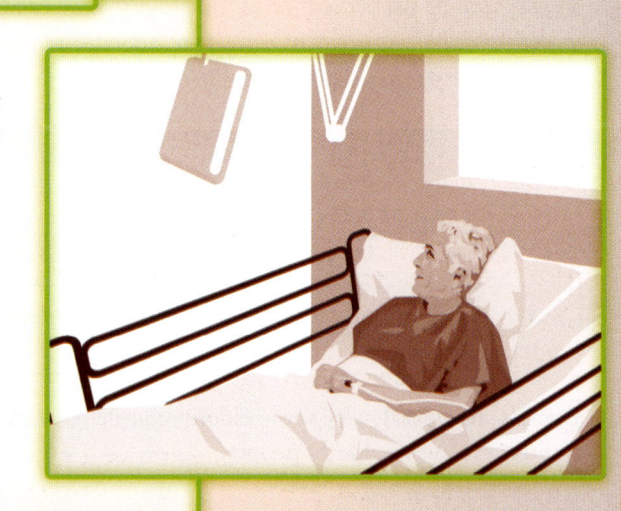

continued

Chapter 5 Changing Society

What you should know – continued

- Some elderly people exercise regularly in order to maintain fitness, while others suffer from weight problems and related illnesses.
- Richer elderly people may be able to afford private health care where they will be treated sooner.
- Some illnesses are often age related, such as Alzheimer's disease. This can have an impact on overall health levels.
- Any other valid point. (Be aware that this is not a complete list. You may think of other possible ideas and examples yourself.)

General question (2007 Q2b)

> Some elderly people are healthier than other elderly people.
>
> Give **two** reasons to explain why some elderly people are healthier than other elderly people.
>
> (KU, 4 marks)

Look out for

Make sure you understand what you are being asked: the reasons why some elderly people are **HEALTHIER** than others.

General answer

An example of **one** paragraph is given below. This is not a complete answer.

> One reason why some elderly people are healthier than other elderly people is because some elderly can afford private health care to treat illnesses they may develop in older age. This means through private health care a person will pay to be seen much quicker by a doctor or consultant at hospital. Any tests to find out the cause of the illness will be done straight away and therefore action, such as medication or surgery, can be carried out to fix the problem. For example, if a person in need of a hip replacement can pay to attend a private hospital they can have the surgery carried out within days.

Complete the rest of the answer yourself. Use the summary and PEE method to help you.

Credit question (2002 Q2a)

> Some elderly people have greater health **needs** than other elderly people.
>
> Explain, **in detail**, why some elderly people have greater health **needs** than other elderly people.
>
> (KU, 6 marks)

This question looks at comparisons between elderly people (those who have greater health needs than others), and the reasons why.

Credit answer

An example of **two** paragraphs are given below. This is not a complete answer.

> One reason why some elderly people have greater health needs than other elderly people is due to the link between poverty and ill health. *Some elderly people live a poorer financial life than others. This means they cannot afford a lifestyle that may improve their health.* For example, elderly people who are financially worse off face issues such as buying the correct types of foods which help keep them healthy. This is because some of these food types such as fruit and vegetables are more expensive than less healthy foods. Because of poverty some elderly cannot afford these foods. Therefore it is evident that due to a lack of money many elderly people, compared to others, cannot afford the sorts of items that can help them live a healthier lifestyle.
>
> An additional reason why some elderly people have greater health needs is because health problems increase with age. *As people grow older they are more likely to experience specific health problems. It then becomes more difficult to recover or fight off these problems.* For example, people who are aged 75 years and over are more likely to suffer from health problems such as arthritis of the bones and dementia than an elderly person who is in their mid-60s. Therefore the person in their 60s is likely to lead a more healthy lifestyle than the person suffering from age related illnesses such as dementia, which can lead to other health problems, such as risk of accidents.

Wealth of the elderly

What you should know…

> The concept being assessed is **equality.** *Why are some elderly wealthier than others?*

An area you can be questioned on at General and Credit levels is 'reasons why some elderly people are wealthier than others'. There is a recap summary to remind you of the main points of this area. Afterwards there are sample questions and answers.

continued

Chapter 5 Changing Society

What you should know – continued

Summary

- Many pensioners rely only on the state pension provided by the Government, which is currently £95·25 per week for a single person. This will make it very difficult for an elderly person to have an adequate standard of living.

- Some elderly people are not aware of the additional benefits they can receive, or are unable to complete the forms, which are sometimes complicated. This means they have a lower standard of living.

- Some elderly people may be wealthier than other elderly people because they have additional pensions to provide extra money. Private and occupational pensions paid into through their working lives give opportunities to buy suitable housing and health care, among other things. Some elderly people, on the other hand, may rely only on their state pension.

- Elderly people may have saved throughout their working lives so they can have a comfortable lifestyle in retirement. This allows them to have the items which meet all their personal needs. Other elderly people may not have had well paid jobs which allowed them to save.

- If home mortgages are paid off through having had a good working wage, elderly people will have free money to spend as they wish. This money could help them to buy high quality care.

- Any other valid point. (Be aware that this is not a complete list. You may think of other possible ideas and examples yourself.)

General questions

> Some elderly people can afford housing that is ideal for their needs.

Give **two** reasons why some elderly people can afford housing that is ideal for their needs. (General 2005 Q2b, 4 marks)

> Some elderly people are wealthier than other elderly people.

Give **two** reasons to explain why some elderly people are wealthier than other elderly people. (General 2009 Q2c, 4 marks)

General answer (2005 Q2b)

An example of **one** paragraph is given below. This is not a complete answer.

> There are many reasons why some elderly people can afford housing that is ideal for their needs. One reason may be that during their working life they were in a position to afford to contribute to an occupational pension. This allows them to have additional money on top of their state pension in their retirement. Using this money they may be able to make the necessary changes to their home which makes it much easier for them to continue living there. For example, an elderly person who worked as a teacher would contribute around 6% of their wage each month into an occupational pension fund. This percentage would be matched by their employer. When the person retired from work this pension would start being paid back to them on a monthly basis.

Use PEE to complete the rest of this answer.

General answer (2009 Q2c)

An example of **one** paragraph is given below. This is not a complete answer.

> One reason why some elderly people are wealthier than others may be that during their working life a person had a well paid job which allowed them to save money each month after all bills and expenses were paid. This would allow them to have this money in their retirement, which they could spend. However some elderly may not have had a well paid job during their working life. This would mean they would not have had any 'spare' money to save for later in life. For example, a well paid worker may have saved £100 per month during their working life of 40 years. This adds up to £48 000 in savings for their retirement.

Use PEE to complete the rest of this answer.

⚠ Look out for

The number of marks awarded to the question.

Chapter 5 Changing Society

The ways the needs of the elderly can be met

What you should know…

> The concept being assessed is **need**. *Who meets the needs of the elderly?*

An area you can be questioned on at General level is 'the ways the needs of the elderly can be met'.

To date this area has not been examined at Credit level. **HOWEVER**, this **does not** mean it will not be examined at some stage in the future.

Below is a recap summary to remind you of the main points of this area. Afterwards there are sample questions and answers.

Summary

The needs of elderly people can be met in a number of ways:

Family

- Family members can meet the needs of elderly people by having them live with them. Children or other family may move the elderly person into their house, to avoid them living alone or in residential care. This helps avoid loneliness and financial strains.
- Family can visit elderly relatives to help avoid loneliness and boredom.
- Family members may help by providing travel assistance so the elderly person can go places and do things they enjoy.
- Family members may help pay housing costs and bills so the elderly person does not need to worry about affording bills, such as heating.
- Any other valid point. (Be aware that this is not a complete list. You may think of other possible ideas and examples yourself.)

Elderly

- Elderly people can remain active and enjoy various interests. This helps keep them physically and mentally active and fit, which can help improve their health and prolong their life.
- Some elderly people may have a wide group of friends and family. This will help them stay active which helps prevent loneliness and depression.
- Any other valid point. (Be aware that this is not a complete list. You may think of other possible ideas and examples yourself.)

continued

What you should know – continued

Government

- The United Kingdom (UK) Government provides all women over 60 and men over 65 years with a state pension. This helps them to pay bills and provide the items they need to live. State pensions are universal benefits (i.e. all adults of this age and above receive the state pension). However, elderly people can apply to defer their pension if they are still working.
- The UK Government provides a Winter Fuel Allowance so that elderly people can pay their heating bills at the coldest times of years. Relying only on their pension means many chose between heating and eating. The WFA means they can now heat their homes and help prevent illness and, in some circumstances, death.
- The UK Government provides free health care, such as operations, medical prescriptions and eye examinations. Also, district nurses will visit elderly patients to tend to medical needs.
- The Scottish Government provides free personal health care to all elderly in Scotland. This means if they require sheltered, residential or nursing care, it will be provided free of charge, unless a person wishes to pay for a higher standard of care.
- The Scottish Government also provides free bus and reduced rail travel costs for elderly people.
- Any other valid point. (Be aware that this is not a complete list. You may think of other possible ideas and examples yourself.)

Voluntary groups/local councils

- Local councils (authorities) provide services such as home helps. This is when a trained worker will spend a period of time each week carrying out tasks for elderly people. They will undertake tasks such as shopping, cleaning, ironing and helping with personal needs such as dressing. Most councils provide this service free of charge; however, some, such as East Dunbartonshire Council, charge a fee.
- Local councils carry out a meals on wheels service. This is when meals are made and delivered to elderly people who may be unable to cook for themselves anymore.
- Voluntary groups, such as Help the Aged, campaign for the rights of elderly people. They try to make sure the Government treat elderly people fairly and that they get all the benefits they are entitled to.
- Voluntary groups run lunch clubs and social trips for elderly people. This provides them with a place to go each day and helps them develop new relationships.
- Any other valid point. (Be aware that this is not a complete list. You may think of other possible ideas and examples yourself. Look at www.ageconcern.org.uk.)

Chapter 5 Changing Society

General questions

There have been two General questions examining this area over the years. Although they are worded differently and deal with various groups such as family or government, they all focus on the same issue: **Meeting the needs of the elderly**.

> The **needs** of some elderly people can be met by their family.
>
> Describe **two** ways in which the **needs** of some elderly people can be met by their family. (General 2003 Q2a, 4 marks)

> The Government tries to help meet the needs of elderly people.
>
> Describe **two** ways in which the Government tries to help meet the needs of elderly people. (General 2007 Q2c, 4 marks)
>
> **To answer this question, you may wish to use the drawings below.**

Look out for

You should notice that these two questions focus on the same area: Meeting the needs of the elderly. The key thing for you to do is identify the issue in the question. Is it asking how the Government helps? Or is it how families, etc., help?

Provided here are the first parts of the answers to each of these two General questions. Your job is to spot the similarities, the differences and complete the answer to each!

General answer (2003 Q2a)

An example of **one** paragraph is given below. This is not a complete answer.

> The needs of some elderly people can be met by their family in many ways. One way is by having the elderly relative living with them. If the elderly person is no longer able to live on their own in their own house, they may not want to live in sheltered or residential accommodation with people they do not know. In order to solve these problems the family may bring them to live with them in their home with the family who they will know in a house which is familiar to them. For example, if a parent cannot cope on their own anymore, their son or daughter may bring them to live with them and their children. This means the elderly person will have the company of their family.

Standard Grade Modern Studies

General answer (2007 Q2c)

An example of **one** paragraph is given below. This is not a complete answer.

> One way the Government tries to meet the needs of the elderly is by providing free medical care. This means that if an elderly person needs medical treatment, such as a prescription, they do not need to pay for it. This helps meet their health needs, as if they are living on a basic state pension of £95·25 per week, they may not go to the doctor for medical treatment if they thought it would cost them money. However, due to prescriptions being free of charge for elderly people, instead of £4·00 (£3·00 from April 2010) that other adults pay, they can receive the necessary medication for conditions such as high blood pressure.

Look out for

Read the newspapers. Reading a newspaper each day (the news sections!) will help you develop an understanding of current concepts, such as equality, and gain valuable examples to use in your answers. All newspapers are now accessible via the internet. For example:

www.herald.co.uk
www.scotsman.com
www.timesonline.co.uk
www.express.co.uk
www.guardian.co.uk

The family

What you should know…

There are three key areas you can be questioned on at General and Credit levels regarding the family in Changing Society.

- The reasons why some families have low living standards or cannot meet their needs.
- The reasons why some parents have difficulty finding a job.
- Policies of the Government for helping families.

Chapter 5 Changing Society

The reasons families struggle to meet their needs

What you should know…

> The concepts being assessed are **need/equality.** *The reasons why needs are not met and some families have more than others.*

An area you can be questioned on at General level is 'why families with children do not all have the same standard of living'. At Credit level it tends to focus on 'the reasons families may be unable to meet the needs of their children'. Although worded differently, both issues focus on the same area; the reasons why some families cannot provide the things they want for their children.

Below is a recap summary to remind you of the main points of this area. Afterwards there are General and Credit sample questions and answers.

Summary

- Different parents have different jobs and income levels. This means some parents may earn a lot more than other parents. This allows them to provide all the necessary items and other luxuries for their children.
- Some families may be unemployed and therefore must survive on a greatly reduced income. This means they may not be able to provide necessary foods or clothing for their children.
- The number of children in the family has an impact on lifestyle and needs being met. Parents with one child will be able to spend more money and time on that child than parents who have five children. They need to divide their spending and time on the children.
- Many families are now lone parent households: some 52% in Scotland. Lone parent families will only have one income, meaning, in all likelihood, less money than a two parent family. Lone parents may also have to work long hours, meaning they see little of their children.
- Some parents may have low educational levels and therefore may not be able to meet the development needs, educationally and/or socially, of their children.
- Any other valid point. (Be aware that this is not a complete list. You may think of other possible ideas and examples yourself.)

Look out for!

The wording of the question. 'Meeting needs' requires you to focus on specific needs, such as development or emotional needs being met. 'Standard of living' requires you to focus upon factors which influence living levels such as income.

Standard Grade Modern Studies

General question (2002 Q2c)

> Families with young children do not all have the same standard of living.

Give **two** reasons why families with young children do not all have the same standard of living.

(KU, 4 marks)

*This question deals with a family's **standard of living**.*

General answer

An example of **one** paragraph is given below. This is not a complete answer.

> One reason why families with young children do not all have the same standard of living is that parents may have different jobs and wage levels. This means that the parents of one family may work in a low skilled, low paid job where they cannot afford to provide their family with all the items they would like. This is different to other families where the parents may be in a high skilled, highly paid job. For example, a parent who is a cleaner receiving a minimum wage of £220 per week, will not be able to afford holidays and new clothes regularly for their children. Whereas a lawyer who earns £1000 per week will be able to afford these things, giving their family a higher standard of living.

You should use the PEE method to complete the rest of this answer.

Credit question (2007 Q2a)

> Some families are unable to meet the needs of their children.

Explain, **in detail**, the reasons why some families are unable to meet the needs of their children.

(KU, 6 marks)

*This question deals with a family's ability to meet the **needs of their children**.*

Chapter 5 Changing Society

Credit answer

An example of **one** paragraph is given below. This is not a complete answer.

> There are a number of reasons why some families are unable to meet the needs of their children. One reason is unemployment. Some families may have parents who are unemployed. As a result of this the family will have a greatly reduced income to live on. They will rely on any savings they have and government benefits. As a result of this parents may not be able to meet their children's dietary needs. They will not be able to buy the correct nutritional food types needed for a healthy diet, as these food types are more expensive. For example, if a parent is unemployed they will receive £63·40 per week in Job Seeker's Allowance. They will receive other benefits such as council tax relief. However, their income will be greatly reduced. This means they cannot buy food items such as fresh meats and fish and fruit and vegetables. Therefore this will impact on their child's dietary health meaning their physical needs are not being met as well as they could be.

Look out for

The number of marks for this question.

Use the PEER technique to complete the rest of this question.

Why do some parents have problems finding a job?

What you should know…

> The concept being assessed is **equality.** Parents having equal opportunities.

An area you can be questioned on at General and Credit levels is 'the reasons why lone parents or parents with young children have difficulty finding a job'.

Below is a recap summary to remind you of the main points of this area. Afterwards there are General and Credit sample questions and answers.

Summary

- Parents can have difficulty finding suitable work due to a lack of childcare. In many areas suitable childcare is difficult to find near to the home.
- Childcare can be very expensive. The Government helps provide all three- and four-year-olds with a nursery and pre-school place. However, for many children aged under three years, parents have to pay for care. Many private nurseries can charge up to £1000 per month for a child.
- Many workplaces do not provide childcare facilities for parents to bring their children. This means workers have to try to make alternative arrangements.
- Many parents have difficulty working evenings or doing overtime or shift work, due to their children. Parents cannot work nights if there is nobody to look after the children.
- Many employers are prejudiced against mothers or single parents as they believe they may leave to have another child or take time off if their child is ill. This makes employers less likely to give them a job.

continued

What you should know – continued

- Many parents may have to fit their working hours around school hours. This makes it more difficult to find suitable employment.
- Any other valid point. (Be aware that this is not a complete list. You may think of other possible ideas and examples yourself.)

General question (2003 Q2b)

> Some lone parents find it more difficult to get a suitable job than other people.

Give **two** reasons why some lone parents find it more difficult to get a suitable job than other people.

(KU, 4 marks)

Make very sure you are aware of the family type the question is asking you about.

General answer

One reason why some lone parents find it more difficult to get a suitable job than other people is because as a lone parent it will be very difficult for them to work evenings or shifts. Finding someone to look after their child in the evenings is harder than during the day. Also, they need to find someone who is flexible, as shifts mean the working hours will change. This makes it harder for the lone parent to find a suitable job. For example, they would be less able to have a job in the police force due to evening and shift work.

A second reason why a lone parent may find it harder is due to the cost of childcare. While the parent is at work they may need someone to look after their child. This can cost a lot of money. The parent has to find care which they can afford and still have enough money for them and their child to live on. For example, a lone parent who works may have to put their child into a summer school in order for them to be looked after. This can cost the parent £50 per week.

Chapter 5 Changing Society

Credit question (2004 Q2b)

> People with young children may have limited job opportunities.

Explain, **in detail**, why people with young children may have limited job opportunities.

(KU, 4 marks)

*Pay close attention to the wording of the question: people with **young children** having limited job opportunities.*

Credit answer

An example of **one** paragraph is given below. This is not a complete answer.

There are many factors which limit the job opportunities of people with young children. One factor is securing a job with suitable working hours. This means that if a parent has no one to care for the child outwith school hours, they are restricted to finding a job which has a working time of approximately 9am to 3pm. This is very difficult to secure as most employers will expect you to be in the workplace until 5pm. If you are unable to do this you have less chance of gaining that job. For example, if a parent applies for an office position with a law firm, the hours of business will be 9am till 5pm, and all staff will be expected to work those hours. If a candidate states they can only work until 3pm for childcare reasons, they are less likely to get the job. Therefore having young children who require care can hamper job prospects due to the hours of care required after school.

Complete the remainder of the answer using the PEER method.

Government policies to help families

What you should know…

> The concept being assessed is **ideology**.
> The ideas to help improve a situation.

An area you can be questioned on at General and Credit levels is 'the ways in which Government policies can help families with children'.

Below is a recap summary to remind you of the main points of this area. Afterwards there are General and Credit sample questions and answers.

continued

What you should know – continued

Summary

Benefits received by families will be means tested.

This means that the money you get depends on:

- how much you've got coming in – your income
- how much you've got in your savings
- What a family's needs are.

Government policies include:

- Educational Maintenance Allowance is provided to encourage children of school leaving age to remain in education and progress their learning, rather than leaving with limiting qualifications. An EMA is a payment of between £10–£30 per week paid to the child of a low income family to help pay the costs of remaining in full time school or college education.
- The National Minimum Wage was established in 1999 to improve the earnings of low paid workers. This improved income can help pay for family issues, such as childcare and household bills.
- Child Tax Credits allow families to receive a Government payment to help with the costs of raising children. Although means tested, nine out of ten families receive CTC. Also, poorer families receive a larger payment.
- Child Benefit is paid to all parents with children aged up to 16 or 19 if still in education. This helps with the costs of raising children. This is a universal benefit (it is paid to all families regardless of income). Look at www.dwp.gov.uk.
- The Child Trust Fund (universal benefit) was set up in 2002. This is a scheme where each child is given £250 from the Government at birth and the same amount on their seventh birthday. Children from poorer families receive more. This money can be added to by families, but it cannot be withdrawn until the child reaches 18 years of age. At this stage the child will have an amount of money which will have increased through interest over the years. Look at www.hmrc.gov.uk/childbenefit.
- The New Deal was established to help unemployed people find a job. This helps people such as parents learn new skills to help them be more employable. Obviously, if parents are in work the family income will be higher.
- Any other valid point. (Be aware that this is not a complete list. You may think of other possible ideas and examples yourself. Look at www.direct.gov.uk.)

General question (2005 Q2a)

> The Government has tried to reduce poverty amongst families.

Describe **two** recent Government policies which try to reduce poverty amongst families.

(KU, 4 marks)

Look out for

The key words in this question are **recent Government policies**. Obviously the question referred to recent policies in 2005.

Chapter 5 Changing Society

General answer

You are going to try this answer yourself!
Set it out in the following method:

> POINT = What is my first policy going to be? Lay it out in a sentence.
>
> EXPLAIN = Explain what the policy does for families and how it helps.
>
> EXAMPLE = Give an example of the policy helping a family. Give a fact, such as 'a £30 per week EMA payment to a child to stay in education can help the child improve their qualifications rather than leaving education to take a low paid job in order to help their family pay the bills'.

Good luck!

Credit question (2009 Q2a)

Government Policies to help Families with Dependent Children (2007)

ema — Education Maintenance Allowance   SureStart   Child Benefit

CHILD TAX CREDITS   Child Trust Fund   new deal

> Government policies help families with dependent children in different ways.

Choose **two** policies from the six above.

For each policy, describe, **in detail**, the ways in which it helps families with dependent children.

(KU, 6 marks)

Look out for

You will not be asked to give arguments for a policy, such as the New Deal. You will be asked to choose a policy and explain how it helps. This means questions such as Credit 2003, Q2a are now not used.

Look out for

The question instructs you how many policies to choose. You must answer on **two** policies in order to gain the full number of marks.

Standard Grade Modern Studies

Credit answer

An example of **one** paragraph is given below. This is not a complete answer.

> The Government has introduced many policies to help families with dependent children. One policy is the Child Trust Fund. This scheme was established for children born on or after 1 September 2002. The Government 'gifted' £250 to the child, with the same amount due on the child's seventh birthday. The benefit of this money is that it cannot be withdrawn until the child reaches 18 years of age. Over this time the fund can be added to by parents and family members, allowing the total in the fund to grow. The fund should also grow with interest over the 18 year period. The child then receives the money at the age of 18. For example, the child may use this money to fund university education in order to improve their employment opportunities in later life. This will help them provide a better financial life for their own family. Without the Child Trust Fund the child's parents may not have had the money to pay for university education. Therefore it is clear that this Government policy can help families with children improve their life circumstances.

Use the PEER method to complete this answer.

Employment

What you should know…

There are three key areas you can be questioned on at General and/or Credit levels with regards to employment in Changing Society.

- The methods used by the Government to help meet the needs of the unemployed.
- The ways in which the Government and other agencies help people find a job.
- The ways in which technology allows people to work from home.

59

Chapter 5 Changing Society

Ways the Government helps meet the needs of the unemployed

What you should know…

> The concepts being assessed are **need and ideology**.
> *The needs of the unemployed, and the ideas to help them.*

*The General recap summary will focus on meeting the needs of the unemployed. The Credit recap summary will look at helping the unemployed **and** low paid workers.*

An area you can be questioned on at General and Credit levels is 'Government methods and policies to help meet the needs of unemployed and/or low paid people'.

Below is a recap summary to remind you of the main points of this area. Afterwards there are General and Credit sample questions and answers.

Summary

General (Meeting the needs of the unemployed)

- The Government provides income benefits such as Job Seeker's Allowance (JSA) to allow people to buy the items they need.
- The Government provides Housing Benefit to help pay rent/mortgages, so that people have a home to live in.
- The Government will establish schemes to attract foreign investment to establish jobs in the UK.
- The Government may give people a grant of money to help them set up their own business.
- The Government has set up training schemes, such as New Deal and Modern Apprenticeships to encourage people to develop their skills in the working world. (Look at www.modernapprenticeships.org.uk).
- Any other valid point. (Be aware that this is not a complete list. You may think of other possible ideas and examples yourself. Look at www.jobcentreplus.gov.uk.)

General question (2002 Q2b)

> There are many ways that the **needs** of unemployed people can be met by the Government.
>
> Describe **two** ways in which the Government helps meet the **needs** of unemployed people.
>
> (KU, 4 marks)

General answer

Below is a sample answer to the question on the previous page. The first part of the answer is done as an example for the first 2 marks. Your job is to complete the answer.

An example of **one** paragraph is given below. This is not a complete answer.

> One way in which the Government helps meet the needs of unemployed people is by attempting to attract new businesses to the UK to help create new jobs. The Government does this by convincing the business that they should set up their factory in a specific area, which might be suffering from high unemployment. The Government will offer rewards or help to pay for the building of the factory. This helps unemployed people as they then have a greater opportunity of securing a job. For example, the Audi car company from Germany recently built their largest sales showroom and mechanic facility in Europe in the Renfrew area, outside Glasgow, an area which suffers from unemployment. The arrival of Audi may have helped provide jobs for some of those unemployed people.

Summary

Credit (Helping the unemployed and low paid workers)

- National Minimum Wage: Was established by the Labour Government in 1999 to ensure people were paid a realistic amount for the work they did. It also made work more appealing than being on benefits. Currently the rate is £5·73 per hour for people aged 22 and over (www.hmrc.gov.uk/nmw).
- The NMW ensured employers could not take advantage of the workers by paying a low hourly rate.
- The NMW also helped remove some people from poverty. It helps groups such as women and ethnic minorities who tend to be low paid or in part time work.
- The New Deal was introduced in 1998 as part of the 'Welfare to Work' strategy to help reduce unemployment and improve the chances of people who had been claiming benefits for at least six months. People will find it easier to secure a job.
- The New Deal gives the unemployed person a personal adviser who works with them to produce CVs, learn interview techniques, develop new skills and enrols them on work experience and training programmes. Therefore it provides a better trained work force.
- Working Tax Credit was established to encourage both parents and non parents to work, rather than rely on benefits. The credit allows workers on low income to pay less tax on their earnings, therefore keeping more money.
- Working Tax Credit also contributes up to 70% towards childcare costs.

continued

Chapter 5 Changing Society

- Child Tax Credit was established to help reduce the levels of child poverty in the UK. It is payable to all couples with a combined income of up to £61 000, including those unemployed.
- Other benefits for the unemployed and people on low incomes include: free prescription charges, free eye tests, free dental care, free school meals and clothing vouchers.
- Any other valid point. (Be aware that this is not a complete list. You may think of other possible ideas and examples yourself.)

Ways the Government and other agencies help people find a job

What you should know…

> The concept being assessed is **ideology**.
> *Ideas to help people find a job.*

An area you can be questioned on at General and Credit levels is 'the methods used by governments and other groups to help people find employment'.

Below is a recap summary to remind you of the main points of this area. Afterwards there are General and Credit sample questions and answers.

Summary

- Governments give grants of money to people to help them start their own business. If an unemployed electrician wishes to start his own business he will need finance to do this (buy equipment, transport, business cards, etc.). Government can provide this.
- Training schemes are in place to improve employable skills, such as Modern Apprenticeships and Skillseekers.
- Modern Apprenticeships offer those over 16 paid employment with training. MAs allow young people to gain skills and qualifications without having to study full time. Many apprentices are kept on by the employer on completion of their training.
- Skillseekers is a training programme for young people who have left school. It provides a work placement where skills are learned.
- Jobcentre Plus helps people find work. Launched in April 2002 it has advisers who provide information about vacancies and can help prepare candidates for interviews.
- The New Deal initiative provides a period of time while receiving benefits to improve skills and experience, making people more employable. Working with a personal adviser, a plan is prepared to help get the person into a suitable job.

continued

What you should know – continued

- Educational Maintenance Allowance was established in 2000 to encourage young people to remain in full-time education. It is a financial payment given to S5/6 pupils of school leaving age, of up to £30 per week. It helps meet their needs while still in education. This means they can enhance their qualifications, making them more employable in the future (www.ema.direct.gov.uk).
- Careers advisers discuss job opportunities with school pupils. They advise on skills and qualifications required for training courses, further education and jobs.
- Work experience placements are set up to allow young people to gain an insight into the world of work. Usually pupils in S4 spend a week in a work environment.
- Any other valid point. (Be aware that this is not a complete list. You may think of other possible ideas and examples yourself.)

General question (2004 Q2a)

> The Government tries to help unemployed people find work.

Describe **two** ways in which the Government tries to help unemployed people find work.

(KU, 4 marks)

General question (2008 Q2a)

> The Government tries to help unemployed people find jobs.

Describe **two** ways in which the Government tries to help unemployed people find jobs.

To answer this question, you may wish to use the drawing above.

(KU, 4 marks)

Chapter 5 Changing Society

General answer (2004 Q2a)

An example of **one** paragraph is given below. This is not a complete answer.

> One way in which the Government tries to help unemployed people find work is through the Modern Apprenticeship Scheme. This is a project partly funded by the Government where young people can gain an apprenticeship and learn on the job training and skills. While doing their training they are paid a wage and attend college, usually one day per week, to help enhance their skills. Often at the end of the three year apprenticeship the person can be kept on by their employer. For example, an 18-year-old school leaver may find a plumbing apprenticeship. Their training and wages are partly paid for by the Government. This gives the person a skilled trade.

Try to complete the rest of this answer using PEE.

! Look out for

Questions appear which are identical. If you are familiar with the questions and have practised them often, it is a very easy way of picking up full marks. The 2008 question on the previous page is identical to the 2004 question we have just answered. The only difference is the word 'work' has been replaced by the word 'jobs'!

Credit question (2005 Q2a)

> Getting a job is a challenge for young people. Many young people need help which is available from Central Government, local councils and voluntary organisations.

Describe **two** different ways in which **either** Central Government **or** local councils **or** voluntary organisations help young people to get a job.

For **each** way, explain why it might be effective in helping a young person get a job.

(KU, 6 marks)

Credit question (2006 Q2a)

Recent Government Policies to improve Employment Opportunities

- new deal
- Skillseekers
- jobcentreplus
- ema Education Maintenance Allowance
- MODERN APPRENTICESHIPS

Choose **two** policies from the list above.

Describe, **in detail**, the ways in which each policy has tried to improve employment opportunities.

(KU, 6 marks)

Credit answer (2006 Q2a)

An example of **one** paragraph is given below. This is not a complete answer.

> One recent Government policy which has tried to improve employment opportunities is the Education Maintenance Allowance. EMA was introduced to give financial help to young people aged 16-19, who have left compulsory education, and who come from lower income backgrounds. The EMA is a payment of up to £30 per week paid directly to the young person allowing them to stay in post-16 education, rather than leave to gain a job to help their family. In many cases this work would be low skilled and low paid, as the qualification of the youngster would not have progressed beyond Standard Grade. Due to them being able to stay in post-16 education they can gain more qualifications and then progress into further education such as university and therefore often higher paid jobs. For example, a university graduate is more likely to gain employment within six months and receive a higher wage than a non university graduate. Therefore the EMA helps improve employment opportunities as it allows young people to stay in education, giving them the chance to enhance their qualifications and therefore have better employment chances in the future.

Use PEER to answer the rest of this question and Q2a, 2005 on the previous page.

Chapter 5 Changing Society

New technology

What you should know…

> The concepts being assessed are **equality and need.**
> *The requirement for new technology in the workplace.*

An area you can be questioned on at General and Credit levels is 'the ways in which technology has allowed some people to work from home and the benefits this brings'.

Below is a recap summary to remind you of the main points of this area. Afterwards there are General and Credit sample questions and answers.

Summary

- The internet allows many people to work from home, as they can send work to a central office or database through e-mail. For example, an accountant can receive and send a client's financial figures in this way. Broadband has now made this a fast and easy way to work.
- The use of mobile phones, such as the Blackberry and iPhone, allows people to send and check e-mails at no extra cost.
- E-bay allows people to buy and sell items online. This is a way to earn money at home.
- Video conferencing allows meetings to take place with colleagues or business contacts from around the world. All that is needed is the internet and a web cam. This cuts down costs and travel. It is cheaper doing this than travelling to Australia!
- The use of skype allows people to talk face to face over the internet.
- Working from home gives flexible working hours. Instead of working 9–5 in an office, you can do the same work at home at a time to suit you. You could work from 12 until 4pm and then from 7 until 11pm if you wished.
- Working from home helps people with young children, as they can combine work with caring for their children. This way childcare costs are not an issue.
- Any other valid point. (Be aware that this is not a complete list. You may think of other possible ideas and examples yourself.)

Standard Grade Modern Studies

General question (2008 Q2b)

Technology has allowed many people to work from home.

Give **two** ways in which technology has allowed many people to work from home.

For **each** way, explain why it has allowed many people to work from home.

To answer this question, you may wish to use the drawing above.

(KU, 4 marks)

General answer

An example of **one** paragraph is given below. This is not a complete answer.

One way in which technology has allowed many people to work from home is through the use of video conferencing with web cameras. This has allowed people to work from home because they can communicate with a colleague or speak with clients face to face using the web camera. All they need is a computer, a broadband internet connection and a web camera. For example, an accountant in his home in Glasgow could speak to a client in London by using his computer and web camera.

Use PEE to complete the rest of the answer.

Chapter 5 Changing Society

Credit question (2005 Q2b)

> Some people prefer to work from home for a variety of reasons. Technology allows them to do this.

Explain, **in detail**, the reasons why some people prefer to work from home.

In answering this question you **must** refer to:

- The needs of some people
- The technology available

(KU, 4 marks)

Credit answer

An example of **one** paragraph is given below. This is not a complete answer.

> There are many reasons why some people prefer to work from home. One reason is due to the fact it is suitable for people with young children, as they do not need to pay for childcare costs. By working from home they can combine the work they do along with caring for their child during the day. They can do work while the child is asleep or playing during the day and then complete the work once the child has gone to bed in the evening. Due to working from home their hours can be flexible in this way. For example, a mother who is an accountant can complete client's accounts at home while caring for her child and then e-mail the finished work to her clients. Therefore working from home helps some people, as they can combine it with other necessary activities.

Use the PEER method to complete the rest of this answer.

REMEMBER, make sure you always think about the concept(s) for each question before you begin your answer.

Ideologies Chapter 6

The USA

What you should know...

When you study Ideologies and Emerging Nations in Syllabus Area 3 you study either the USA or China. For the purposes of this book, we will focus only on the USA as this is the area mainly studied by Standard Grade candidates.

There are five areas you can be questioned on at General and/or Credit level Knowledge and Understanding (KU) when studying the USA.

- The rights and responsibilities American citizens have.
- The political rights and responsibilities of citizens.
- The ways citizens can participate in elections and the reasons why they participate (including ethnic minority participation).
- The ways in which the American Dream shapes lives.
- The inequalities which exist between ethnic groups in the USA and how they have changed.

Look out for

The terms USA and America will both be used. They mean the same.

Look out for

Use the wording in the question to help you with your answer.

The rights and responsibilities of the American people

What you should know...

The concept being assessed is **rights and responsibilities**. *The rights and responsibilities of American citizens.*

An area you can be questioned on at General Knowledge and Understanding (KU) level is 'the rights and responsibilities that American citizens have'. So far this has not been questioned at Credit level. **HOWEVER**, this **does not** mean it will not be examined at some stage in the future.

Below is a recap summary to remind you of the main points. Following this is a KU General sample question and answer to help you complete this area.

continued

Chapter 6 Ideologies

What you should know – continued

Summary

- Citizens have the right to vote for a candidate of their choice in an election, such as a Presidential election. The responsibility is to use their vote in a correct fashion and not spoil their vote.

- The right to join a political party of their choice, such as the Republican Party. The responsibility is to accept the decisions the party reaches (www.republicans.org, www.democrats.org).

- Citizens have the right to stand in a political election, such as for mayor or governor. The accompanying responsibility is to accept the result of the election, good or bad.

- The right to own a firearm (gun) is given to the American people. The responsibility is not to conceal their weapon in public or use it in an aggressive manner.

- The right to protest against a Government law. The responsibility is not to break the law when carrying out this protest.

- The right to freedom of speech is given to all citizens. However, a person should not give false information or rubbish the character of another person.

- The right to a fair trial is in the American constitution's bill of rights. The responsibility is to tell the truth under oath and not to interfere in the legal case.

- Any other valid point. (Be aware that this is not a complete list. You may think of other possible ideas and examples yourself. Look at www.whitehouse.gov, www.usccr.gov.)

*If asked for **both** rights and responsibilities you **must** include arguments for both.*

General question (2007 Q3a)

> People in the USA have many rights. They also have responsibilities that go with them.

Describe **one** right that American people have.

Describe **one** responsibility that American people have.

In your answer you **must** use American examples.

(KU, 4 marks)

*You are clearly told to focus on **both** rights and responsibilities. Use the question as a guide.*

70

General answer

One right American people have, is the right to vote in an election. This is when the US citizen registers to vote and on election day votes for the political candidate of their choice. For example, in November 2008 many people voted for Barack Obama, the Democratic Party candidate as their choice for President of the USA.

The responsibility that goes with the right to vote is that people use their vote correctly and do not spoil their paper. This means they place an X next to the candidate they wish to win. They do not vote for every candidate or write all over their paper, as this would make it invalid. For example, if someone voted for both Barack Obama and John McCain in the Presidential election, their vote would be spoilt and would not be counted, as you can only choose one candidate.

The political rights and responsibilities of citizens

What you should know…

> The concept being assessed is **rights and responsibilities**. *The political rights and responsibilities of American citizens.*

An area you can be questioned on at both General and Credit levels is 'the political rights and responsibilities of citizens'.

Below is a recap summary to remind you of the main points. Following this are General and Credit sample questions and answers to help you complete this area.

Election day in the USA

Summary

Many of the political rights and responsibilities were covered in the previous section '**The rights and responsibilities of the American people**'. You can use these, as they are politically based. However there are also other political rights and responsibilities:

- American citizens have the right to join an interest group to campaign and put pressure on the Government. The accompanying responsibility is not to intimidate or use violence against people.

- People have the right to freedom of speech and press. This allows them to voice their opinion on an issue and to use the press to get their view across to a wider audience of people. However, they must not be prejudiced or give false information in their work.

- Any other valid point. (Be aware that this is not a complete list. You may think of other possible ideas and examples yourself. Look at www.usa.gov.)

Chapter 6 Ideologies

General question (2005 Q3a)

> American people have political rights and responsibilities.

Describe **one** political right which American people have **and** the responsibility that goes with it.

In your answer, you **must** refer to American examples.

(KU, 4 marks)

*Pay close attention to this instruction. If you don't refer to American examples, you **will not** gain full marks.*

General question (2006 Q3a)

> The American people can use the media to criticise the Government.

Describe **two** ways that the American people can use the media to criticise the Government.

In your answer you **must** use American examples.

(KU, 4 marks)

General answer (2005 Q3a)

One political right American people have is the right to freedom of speech and to use the press. This is when they can voice their opinion over a political decision which has been made by the Government. If they do not agree with the decision they can give their view and use the media to inform others of their disagreement with the Government. For example, if a citizen is not happy at the Obama Government sending more troops to Afghanistan, they could send a letter to the New York Post newspaper to give their opinion which other people may agree with.

However with this right comes the responsibility of ensuring that the person does not give false information or give an opinion which is biased or threatening. This means that their view must be thought out and they do not distort information. For example, they could not say that President Obama is wrong to send more troops to Afghanistan as it leads to a high death rate if that is not statistically true. A citizen also cannot threaten President Obama simply because they do not agree with his decision.

You should notice that, although worded differently, General questions 3a from both 2005 and 2006 can be very similar in their answer. Using the media is a political right. Using the media to criticise the Government is also a political right. Sometimes you have to look beyond what the question asks. Always make sure you recognise what the concept is. This will greatly help you form your answer.

Standard Grade Modern Studies

Credit question (2002 Q3a)

> The American people have **rights and responsibilities**.

Describe, **in detail**, the **political rights** of American people **and** the **responsibilities** that go with them.

In your answer you **must** refer to American examples.

(KU, 8 marks)

Credit question (2006 Q3a)

> In the USA, citizens have both political rights and the responsibilities that go with them.

Describe, **in detail**, the **political rights** of American citizens and the **responsibilities** that go with them.

In your answer you **must** use American examples.

(KU, 8 marks)

Look out for

Notice that some questions are exactly the same. These two questions are identical. The wording is practically the exact same and they are worth the same marks. If you can provide an answer to one of the questions, you can do it for both of them!

Credit answer (2006 Q3a)

An example of **two** paragraphs are given below. This is not a complete answer.

One political right American citizens have is the right to stand as a candidate in a political election. This is when a citizen, who will probably be a member of a political party, decides to stand as an official candidate either in a local, state or national election. For example, Hillary Clinton of the Democratic Party stood for election and was successfully chosen as the state senator for New York, firstly in November 2000. She remained a senator until her cabinet appointment as Secretary of State in 2008. She represented the state and people of New York in the Senate assembly. As the USA is a democratic nation, where the people have power, being a political representative is a key way of exercising their rights.

The responsibility which accompanies the right to stand as a candidate is to accept the final decision of the voters. This means that a candidate must accept that they may not be the person that the people of their area or nation wish to have representing them. They should not challenge a fair result or refuse to accept the leadership of another individual. For example in the 2008 Presidential election, John McCain, the defeated candidate had to accept the result for the good of the American nation. If he had challenged the result, it would have led to problems and a weakening of the American democratic process. Therefore it is important that the responsibility of candidacy is followed in order to allow the political system to operate effectively.

Now you try to complete the rest of this answer using PEER.

Chapter 6 Ideologies

The ways citizens can participate in elections

What you should know…

> The concept being assessed is **participation**. *The ways American citizens can participate in American elections.*

An area you can be questioned on at General and Credit levels is 'the ways people can participate in political elections and the reasons why they participate'.

Below is a recap summary to remind you of the main points. Following this are sample questions and answers to help you complete this area.

A democratic Party rally

Summary (Ways of Participating)

- Citizens can participate by voting in elections. Citizens must first complete a registration form. After they are registered, they can vote in elections, such as for state governor.
- Joining a political party. Citizens with a political interest will join a political party. Many work for the party and progress through various positions.
- Standing for election at local, state, federal or presidential level. Arnold Schwarzenegger stood for and became governor of California.
- Joining an interest group. Citizens who feel strongly about a Government decision or a particular issue such as abortion rights may join an interest group in order to exercise pressure on the decision makers.
- Lobbying and campaigning against or in favour of Government decisions. People campaign in order to publicise their views, such as the Million Moms March, where mothers who have lost children to guns protest against firearm ownership.
- Exercising the right to use the media to give opinions, such as writing to USA Today about the Federal Government policy on the War on Terror.
- Any other valid point. (Be aware that this is not a complete list. You may think of other possible ideas and examples yourself. Look at www.americanpresidents.org.)

Summary (Reasons for Participating)

- People should participate as they will help choose the people who will make decisions for their country. It is the people who chose Barack Obama as the 44th President.
- If a person does not participate in elections they may gain a representative they did not wish or whose political opinions and decisions they do not agree with.
- Many people are encouraged to vote if they have role models. If ethnic minority groups wish to see more of their group in Senate or the White House they have a responsibility to help get them there by voting for them. Obama standing for the Presidency encouraged more black people to vote.
- Any other valid point. (Be aware that this is not a complete list. You may think of other possible ideas and examples yourself.)

Standard Grade Modern Studies

General question (2009 Q3a)

American people can **participate** in politics in many ways.

Describe **two** ways in which American people can **participate** in politics in the USA.

In your answer, you **must** use American examples.

To answer this question, you may wish to use the drawings above.

(KU, 4 marks)

General answer

One way American people can participate in politics in the USA is by standing as a candidate for election. This is when a person will receive their party's nomination or will stand as an independent candidate in order to gain the votes of the public. For example, Charlie Crist stood as the Republican Party candidate for the position of governor of Florida in 2006. He was successful in the election and gained the most votes to become governor.

A second way people can participate in politics is by joining a political party. This is when a person joins a party and plays a role in the work of the party. They may become a fundraiser or canvasser. For example, the Democratic Party spent over $730 million dollars on Barack Obama's successful Presidential campaign. This money had to be raised and was done so by party members who organised events and business donations.

Charlie Crist, Governor of Florida state

75

Chapter 6 Ideologies

Credit question (2008 Q3a)

> American citizens can **participate** in politics in many ways.

Describe, **in detail**, the ways in which American citizens can **participate** in politics.

In your answer, you **must** use American examples.

(KU, 8 marks)

Credit question (2004 Q3a)

> American citizens can participate in elections.

Describe, **in detail**, the ways in which American citizens can participate in elections.

In your answer you **must** refer to American examples of participation in elections.

(KU, 8 marks)

Credit answer (2004 Q3a)

An example of **one** paragraph is given below. This is not a complete answer.

> American citizens can participate in elections in many various ways. One way is by registering to vote in an election. In America citizens must complete a registration form in order to be able to vote. This is a key way of participating as it ensures as many people as possible vote, giving as fair and as representative a result as possible. For example in the recent 2008 Presidential election the number of people registered to vote was nearly 170 million people compared to 136 million who were registered in the 2006 federal elections. Therefore registering to vote is a significant way of participating in elections as it helps fairly select the people who the public want elected. If you are not registered to vote then you cannot vote for the person you want to represent you.

- POINT = State the point (way) that people can participate in elections.
- EXPLAIN = Explain the way that they participate through the point you have made.
- EXAMPLE = Give a relevant example which supports the explanation.
- RELATE = You must then relate the explanation and example back to the original point in order to show that it is a way of participating.
- **REMEMBER:** It is just like going all the way round the clock face, as we discussed in Chapter 3.

Look out for

The subtle difference between the 2009 General and 2004 Credit questions. Although they both focus on political participation, the Credit question examines **elections**. This means you can only deal with participating in elections; therefore you **cannot** include answers such as fundraising or attending party events, as they do not focus on political elections. Also the 2009 General and 2008 Credit questions are identical, apart from the number of marks. However, for the Credit question you must give a more detailed explanation and a relevant up-to-date example. The key difference is ensuring you relate the explanation and example back to the point, in order to prove it is a valid point to make.

Complete the rest of this answer by using the PEER method.

What you should know…

Ethnic minority group participation

This has not been examined at General level. **HOWEVER**, this **does not** mean it will not be examined at some stage in the future.

More and more people, particularly ethnic minority groups, are now more likely to participate in politics. There are a variety of reasons for this:

- Increase in role models. Ethnic minority groups now have people in politics to look up to. People such as Barack Obama becoming the first non-white President gives people inspiration to see change and the belief that others can follow in his footsteps. Also, Condoleeza Rice was an African American woman who held the post of Secretary of State in the George W. Bush administration.

- Ethnic minority celebrities have become heavily involved in political campaigns in recent years. If people such as Will Smith and Oprah Winfrey appear at political rallies, support candidates and encourage people to vote, there is a higher chance of ordinary citizens listening to their message. For example, Oprah Winfrey, America's most successful female celebrity was a huge supporter of Obama's campaign. She encouraged African Americans to vote for Obama.

- There has been an increase in the number of ethnic minority members entering politics. For example, in 2002 there were no African American or Hispanic members in the US Senate. In 2009 the number was three. This increase encourages ethnic minorities to participate as they have greater confidence that a member of their ethnic group will represent their wishes correctly.

- There has been a significant increase in the black middle class. Greater educational attainment has led to more African Americans graduating college and registering to vote. Due to this increasing class status there is a greater interest in what politicians are doing to represent their interests, jobs, savings, etc.

- Ethnic minority groups now make up a greater percentage of the population. Due to this rise they have a greater role in job markets, business and education. They have a greater interest in what the Government will do to help them. For example, in 2000, the major ethnic composition of the USA was 72% White, 12% African American and 12% Hispanic. By early 2009 it had changed to 67% White, 13% African American and 15% Hispanic.

- Particular cities or states often have a high concentration of a particular ethnic minority group living there. This increases the likelihood of the group turning out to vote as there is a belief there is a greater chance of electing a minority candidate from the same ethnic group as themselves. For example, Hawaii has a large Asian and Pacific Islander population (approximately 45% of all citizens) and there is an API senator, Daniel Inouye, representing the state. (Look at www.senate.gov.)

- Any other valid point. (Be aware that this is not a complete list. You may think of other possible ideas and examples yourself.)

Barack Obama, President of the USA

Chapter 6 Ideologies

Credit question (2007 Q3a)

> Ethnic minority groups are now more likely to participate in politics in the USA.

Explain, **in detail**, the reasons why ethnic minority groups are now more likely to participate in politics in the USA.

In your answer, you **must** use American examples.

(KU, 8 marks)

Look out for

Notice that the question examines ethnic **minority** groups.

Answer this question on your own using the PEER method.

REMEMBER:

POINT = State the point (reason) why ethnic minority groups are now more likely to participate in politics. For example, increase in ethnic minority role models.

EXPLAIN = Explain the way that this has helped improve participation through the point you have made.

EXAMPLE = Give a relevant example which supports the explanation. For example, role models, such as Oprah Winfrey and Beyoncé, supporting Barack Obama, gives a positive encouraging message.

RELATE = You must then relate the explanation and example back to the original point in order to show that it is a way of participating in this case. For example, an increase in the number of African American candidates/representatives encourages other people to think that they too can participate in politics, whether by simply voting or running for office themselves.

The American Dream shaping lives

What you should know…

> The concept being assessed is **ideology**.
> *The ideas which help shape success.*

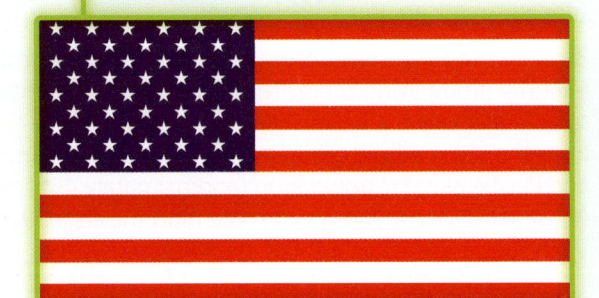

An area you can be questioned on at General level is 'the ways in which the American Dream and the economy of the USA have allowed American people to become rich and successful'. This has not been examined at Credit level. **HOWEVER**, this **does not** mean it will not be examined at some stage in the future.

Below is a recap summary to remind you of the main points of this area. There will then be sample questions and answers for you to study and complete.

continued

78

What you should know – continued

Summary

- The American Dream is the idea that if you work hard you can be successful and wealthy. You can achieve the dream by studying hard at school, which allows you to graduate and attend college. This then allows you to successfully enter the job market.

- As the US has a capitalist economy, people are allowed to retain much of their wealth, due to low taxes. They are also encouraged to start their own businesses. Working hard and establishing your own business (consider Bill Gates with Microsoft and Steve Jobs with Apple), allows you to become extremely rich and successful. This success allows you to employ other American citizens, therefore helping share capitalism and wealth and increasing standards of living.

- Due to the strong economic position of the USA, which has one of the wealthiest economies in the world, it encourages people to be successful.

- Due to the high levels of competition between business, such as Gap and Abercrombie & Fitch in the clothing market, prices can be kept low and quality levels high. Each competitor knows that if one of these categories slips, they will lose business. This competition is good for the customer.

- Affirmative action policies have helped groups such as women and ethnic minorities become more successful in employment, education and politics. People such as Hillary Clinton, Oprah Winfrey and Ralph Alvarez, president of McDonald's, are examples of these groups gaining success.

- Any other valid point. (Be aware that this is not a complete list. You may think of other possible ideas and examples yourself.)

General questions

There are a number of General questions that have been examined on the theme of the American Dream and gaining wealth and success.

> Give **two** reasons why it is possible for some Americans to become rich and successful. (General 2002 Q3b, 4 marks)

> The economy of the USA allows some American people to have high living standards.
>
> Describe **two** ways in which the economy of the USA allows some American people to have high living standards.
>
> In your answer you **must** use American examples. (General 2003 Q3a, 4 marks)

Chapter 6 Ideologies

Many American people have started up their own business.

Give **two** reasons why many American people have started up their own business.

In your answer you **must** refer to American examples. (General 2005 Q3b, 4 marks)

In recent years, many members of ethnic minority groups in the USA have seen an improvement in their standards of living.

Give **two** reasons to explain why many members of ethnic minority groups in the USA have seen an improvement in their standards of living.

In your answer you **must** use American examples. (General 2006 Q3c, 4 marks)

To answer this question, you may wish to use the drawing above.

Give **two** reasons to explain why many American people have become rich and successful.

In your answer you **must** use American examples. (General 2007 Q3c, 4 marks)

Starting up a business can improve the lives of some Americans.

MAX's TYRES
BALANCING • REPAIRS

MAX'S SALES FIGURES

MAX'S TYRES
Balance Sheet
Sales: $550,000
Profit: $240,000
Tax: $ 25,000

Describe **two** ways in which starting up a business can improve the lives of some Americans.

In your answer you **must** use American examples.

To answer this question, you may wish to use the drawings above.

(General 2008 Q3a, 4 marks)

It is very clear that this is a favourite area for examination questions. Six General questions in the last eight years have focused on aspects of the American Dream and capitalism. However, if you take a close look at the questions, you should notice that some have similarities between them:

There has been a focus on asking you to explain the reasons why Americans can become rich and successful.

There has been a focus on asking you to explain the reasons why Americans want to start their own business.

And finally there has been a focus on asking you to explain the ways in which Americans can have a high standard of living.

This shows that although you might think there are lots of questions that can be asked on this area, i.e. six questions, the reality is these questions are in three categories. Although they are worded slightly differently, if two or more questions belong to the same category, then you are being questioned on the same issue, such as improving living standards.

We will now have a look at three of the questions and attempt to answer them.

Chapter 6 Ideologies

General answer (2007 Q3c)

One reason to explain why many American people have become rich and successful is because America has a capitalist approach to its economy. This encourages people to work hard and make as much money and success for themselves as possible. This has allowed many people to start their own business and become successful. As they have progressed it has allowed them to expand their business, giving others the opportunity to work hard and gain wealth and success. For example, Microsoft was established by Bill Gates and Paul Allen. They saw a gap in the computing market for ways to word process and store documents and files. Through their hard work and skill they developed Microsoft Office, a system that a huge number of the world's schools, offices and businesses now use and have done for many years. This has allowed these two men to become multi billionaires.

A second reason which can explain why American people have become rich and successful is due to the high levels of competition which exist in the American business market. Businesses are allowed to compete against each other for customers and income. This means that they will always try to ensure high quality products and competitive prices. This allows them to keep a share of the market. For example, Coca Cola and Pepsi are two soft drink companies who compete against each other. Their products are sold throughout America and worldwide. In order to compete against each other they must make sure their products are always to a high standard and are reasonably priced. If they do this they can share the market and make sure their owners and workers make money and are successful.

General answer (2005 Q3b)

An example of **one** paragraph is given below. This is not a complete answer.

Many American people have started their own business because it is seen as a part of the American Dream. The Dream allows people to be successful and wealthy if they work hard. It allows people to have freedom, opportunities and equality. Part of this is for an American to be able to start their own business and try to work hard and gain success. For example Jerry Jones was able to develop his oil company, Jones Oil and Land Lease, based in Arkansas, which helped him become a very successful business owner. This then allowed him to buy the Dallas Cowboys NFL team, which has proved very successful for the city of Dallas in Texas.

Jerry Jones, Texan businessman

Use the summary, any course notes and the PEE method to help you complete the rest of this answer.

General answer (2006 Q3c)

An example of **one** paragraph is given below. This is not a complete answer.

> Many members of ethnic minority groups in the USA have seen an improvement in their standards of living because they have received greater opportunities in education. Due to the increasing African American middle class, many students are able to attend schools in better off areas with greater resources and teaching staff. Due to better education many ethnic minority students go on to gain a good job with higher pay levels meaning they can afford a better standard of living for themselves and their children in the future. For example, the percentage of African American students who graduated from high school in 2001 was 50%. This increased to approximately 53% by 2008. Therefore this increase shows more people from this ethnic group are gaining higher qualifications, which can help them achieve a higher standard of living.

An African American college graduate

Use the summary, any course notes and the PEE method to help you complete the rest of this answer.

Also, try to answer the other questions where an example is not provided.

Inequalities between ethnic groups in the USA

What you should know…

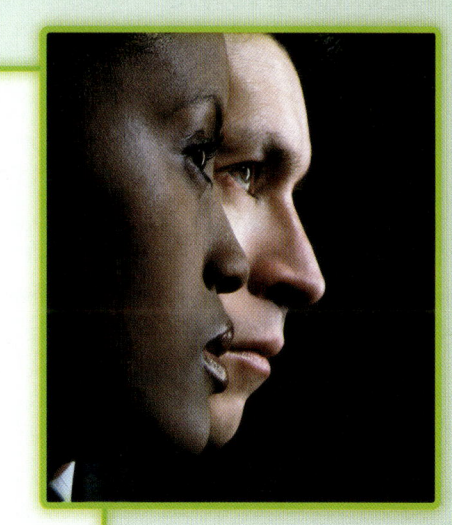

> The concept being assessed is **equality**. *The life differences between groups of people.*

An area you can be questioned on at General and Credit levels is 'the social and economic inequalities that exist in the USA'. This area of questioning will take different forms:

- The reasons why social and economic inequalities exist and the reasons why they are continuing to do so.
- The reasons why unequal treatment exists between ethnic groups and people within the same group in areas such as health, education, crime, etc.

Following is a recap summary to remind you of the main points of this area on inequalities. For simplicity, however, we will split the summary into two, one area for each of the above bullet points. Following this there are sample questions and answers appropriate to these areas.

continued

What you should know – continued

Summary (Social and Economic Inequalities)

- Blacks and Hispanics are more likely to live in poorer housing due to lower educational levels and poorer income. This poorer housing tends to be in areas of deprivation and crime.

- There is a higher level of single parent families among groups such as African Americans. This means fewer opportunities to gain employment and lower incomes than two parent families.

- Black and Hispanic groups are less likely to have health insurance than white people. This means they are less able to receive and pay for necessary health care. There is a reliance on Medicare for people aged over 65 and Medicaid, which is assisted payment for health care. However this care is not as good as the care given to people with insurance. Hispanics are the group least likely to have health insurance. (Look at www.cms.hhs.gov.)

- Approximately 46 million American citizens do not have health insurance and another 25 million are under insured, according to government figures.

- Black Americans have the highest death rates, reducing their life chances and what they can provide for their family.

- Asians have a higher success rate in school and college than all other ethnic groups. For example, approximately 45% of Asian students graduate college, compared to 26% of white students. This means there is a greater chance of obtaining a good job.

- Nearly half of all murder victims in the USA are African American. Over half of all prisoners are African American. This means that people in this ethnic group have a higher likelihood of being involved in crime, reducing life chances and job prospects.

- For those people who are unemployed there is little Government help, with low welfare benefits. This is due to the capitalist American Dream philosophy.

- Any other valid point. (Be aware that this is not a complete list. You may think of other possible ideas and examples yourself. Look at www.uscis.gov.)

What you should know – continued

Summary (Unequal Treatment)

- Black and Hispanic groups are less likely to own their own home. This means they may move around more often. This means fewer job opportunities and disruption to their children's schooling.

- The level of infant mortality for African Americans is almost double the level for white children. These inequalities exist due to a lack of adequate health care/cover and poor housing.

- African Americans have a higher percentage of AIDS/HIV sufferers and deaths than whites. This contributes to an inability to work.

- Some ethnic minority groups face prejudice in areas such as education. There is a lack of investment in schools in poorer areas where minorities tend to be based. For example, additional Government funding is approximately 60 cents per pupil in an inner city ghetto school. In a wealthy suburban school, however, the funding is closer to $10 per pupil. This has an impact on the quality of education provided.

- The better teachers find jobs in better resourced middle class schools. This impacts on learning and therefore educational achievement. Also there is a greater ratio of pupils per teacher in inner city schools. This makes it harder for the teacher to spend as much time with each pupil.

- Any other valid point. (Be aware that this is not a complete list. You may think of other possible ideas and examples yourself.)

An Hispanic American

General question (2002 Q3a)

| Housing | Health | Crime and Justice |

Choose **one** of the topics listed above.

Describe **two** ways in which some members of **ethnic minority groups** in the USA are not treated **equally** in the topic you have chosen.

In your answer you must refer to ethnic minorities in the USA that you have studied.

(KU, 4 marks)

Chapter 6 Ideologies

General question (2004 Q3a)

| Education | Housing | Health |

Choose **one** of the topics from the box above.

Give **two** reasons why some members of **ethnic minority groups** often do less well than white Americans in the topic you have chosen.

In your answer, you must refer to ethnic minority groups in the USA that you have studied.

(KU, 4 marks)

General question (2008 Q3c)

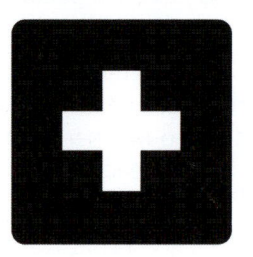

Education   Housing   Health

Some Americans are worse off than others.

Choose **one** of the issues from the box above.

For the issue you have chosen, give **two** reasons why some Americans are worse off than others.

In your answer you **must** use American examples.

(KU, 4 marks)

The three questions are very similar in a number of ways. The concept of **equality** is the same. The questions look at similar areas. Also, they deal with some people being unequal/worse off than others. Therefore the answers should be very similar.

We will look at an answer to one of the questions.

Look out for

The 2002 and 2004 questions are very similar. They focus on ethnic minority groups doing less well or being less fairly treated. This is very similar. Also two of the three topics for you to choose from are the same. **HOWEVER** the difference is that Q3a from 2004 asks you to make a comparison with the white ethnic group. This means you must have an understanding of the reasons why white Americans do well and succeed. You are comparing and contrasting the two groups.

Look out for

The difference between this 2008 question and the 2004 question. The 2008 question discusses **AMERICANS** in general. It does not focus on a specific group. This means you can answer on the elderly, white Americans, Native Americans, non-English speaking Americans and so on.

General answer (2004 Q3a)

> One reason why some members of ethnic minority groups do less well than white Americans in health is because many minority members do not have health insurance to pay for health care. As the cost can be very high, people take out insurance which they pay on a monthly basis. This means that when medical treatment is required the insurance covers the cost. However many people from ethnic minority groups are less likely to have this insurance. This may be because they have a lower income. For example, in 2007 the average Hispanic household had an average income of just over $38 000, whereas white households had an average of $52 000. This lower level means Hispanic people are less likely to be able to afford health insurance.
>
> A second reason why some ethnic minority groups often do less well regarding health is due to the large number of lone parent families which tend to exist. This impacts on health as lone parent families have a lower income to pay for health care insurance. Also there tends to be higher levels of poor housing and poverty in one parent families, meaning they can suffer health problems. For example 57% of all African American families are lone parent led, compared to 22% of white families.

Can you see that there has been a comparison made between ethnic minority groups and the white group?

Try to answer the other General questions relating to inequalities by using the PEE method. Or even answer each question but answer on a different issue each time! Go on, try it!

Credit question (2003 Q3a)

> Social inequality exists in areas such as housing, health, education and the justice system in the USA.

Give **detailed** examples to show that **social** inequalities exist in the USA.

In your answer you **must** refer to American examples.

(KU, 6 marks)

Credit question (2005 Q3a)

> There continues to be social and economic inequality in the USA.

Explain, **in detail**, why there is **social and economic inequality** in the USA.

In your answer, you **must** use American examples.

(KU, 8 marks)

Chapter 6 Ideologies

Credit question (2009 Q3a)

> In the USA, social and economic inequalities continue to exist.

Explain, **in detail**, why in the USA, social and economic inequalities continue to exist.

In answering this question, you must:
- Describe the inequalities which exist.
- Explain the reasons why they exist.

In your answer, you **must** use American examples.

(KU, 8 marks)

Credit answer (2009 Q3a)

An example of **two** paragraphs is given below. This is not a complete answer.

> Key: (1) Describes the inequality. (2) Explains why it exists.
>
> The USA is a nation which has many inequalities. These inequalities contribute to the continuing social and economic differences which exist. One inequality which exists in the USA is in the area of health care. (1) Some minority groups have poorer health. There are huge inequalities between people, as many cannot afford to pay for adequate health care provision. Many people suffer from poor health and disease, because they are unable to receive treatment or because of the quality of treatment they receive. Black Americans for example have the highest death rate in the USA, in part due to poor health and an inability to fund their care. (2) In the USA many people have health insurance to pay for their treatment. Those who can afford the insurance will receive appropriate treatment to a high standard and crucially will be treated in a satisfactory time period. Those people who cannot afford insurance rely on Medicare and Medicaid, which is a public funded health system. However this system has limited resources and often poorer services. For example African Americans and Hispanics are the least likely to have health insurance. An income of $36 000 per household for African Americans and $38 000 for Hispanic families may help explain their limitations where health insurance is concerned. Therefore health is a key area of inequality, as those who can afford to pay, receive better care.

Look out for

The wording of Q3a for 2005 and 2009 are very similar. You answer on the same issues. Basically you are being asked 'why does social and economic inequality exist?' The difference in 2009 is that you are given helpful hints. Use them! You **must** give detailed descriptions of some of the inequalities which exist and the reasons why they exist. If you do not complete these two steps you will **not** receive full marks. If answers do not include examples you will receive a maximum of 5 marks.

A further explanation as to why social and economic inequalities continue to exist can be found in the area of employment. **(1)** The inequality which exists is the varying income levels that different people have. Often this is due to the levels of educational success which exist between people and between ethnic groups. The ability to graduate from school and further education impacts on a person's job chances. **(2)** The better the job a person can secure the more likely they are to receive an income which allows them to provide for themselves and their family. Some groups in the USA are unable to do this. For example, the Asian and Pacific Island ethnic group are the most likely to graduate high school with almost 80% graduating. The Hispanic group is least likely to graduate high school with around 50%. API households earn almost twice as much money on average per year, with $66 000, than Hispanic families earn. It could be argued that this is because of success in education. Therefore it is clear that employment and to a large extent education have a significant effect on the continuing social and economic inequalities which continue to exist in the USA.

You should see where the two bullet points of the question have been answered. You must describe the inequality which exists. After you have done this, and explained why it is an inequality, you must give the reasons why it exists. For the purpose of understanding this answer the two bullet points have been labelled in blue to let you see where they have been answered.

Attempt to provide a third, fourth paragraph to complete this answer.

Remember still to base your answer on the PEER method.

Often, the USA is the area students find most difficult. They feel there is so much they can be examined on. This is a bit of a misconception. You can see there are five key areas for examination questions. This is not a huge number. It is manageable. The area that is large and sometimes difficult to cope with is the **inequalities** area. However, if you can have a knowledge and understanding of the following key areas you should confidently be able to answer this section:

- The inequalities which exist between groups in America (education, health, housing, crime, employment).
- The reasons why these inequalities exist.
- The improvements that have recently been made to narrow the levels of inequality.

Chapter 7 International Relations

Politics of aid

Politics of aid

What you should know…

There are four key areas you can be questioned on at General and/or Credit levels with regard to types of aid given to meet the needs of some African countries:

- Ways in which United Nations aid policies help meet the needs of countries in Africa.
- Political, social and economic factors that **developed** nations consider before they give aid.
- The reasons why some people feel aid does not meet the needs of those who need it the most.
- Reasons why certain issues may prevent African governments from meeting its people's needs; for example, AIDS/HIV, war, drought.

You should be aware of the content Knowledge and Understanding (KU) surrounding **all** these possible question types. There are exemplar KU questions and answers provided later in the chapter.

However, in order to help you make a start, study the summary information on United Nations aid agencies and the General and Credit questions and answers that follow.

UN aid agencies

What you should know…

There are a number of specialised agencies of the United Nations who try to meet the needs of African countries.

> The concept being assessed is **need**. *You should know that some countries need aid (help) in order for its people to survive.*

An area you can be questioned on at both General and Credit levels is 'ways in which United Nations aid policies help meet the needs of countries in Africa'.

We have provided a recap summary to remind you of the main aid agencies. Afterwards there are examples of General and Credit KU questions and answers.

Standard Grade Modern Studies

What you should know…

WHO (World Health Organisation)

The World Health Organisation is there to meet medical needs by promoting good health, health education and providing improved medical facilities. WHO have been involved in many initiatives in Africa including:

- Helping governments set up health services, such as in Sudan who in 2008 established its first mental health clinic.
- Training health professionals, such as doctors, midwives, nurses, etc. In 2006, there were 33 354 midwife and nursing personnel in Sudan.
- Developing primary health care at local village level where hospitals and doctors are not available. For example, in 2006, WHO helped rebuild 197 basic health centres in Madagascar. This greatly helped as 40% of people have no primary health access.
- Researching and working on health problems. In 2007 in Sudan, WHO attempted to manage polio through a 'keep Sudan polio free' campaign. The campaign's coverage results in 2007, showed that 8 910 641 children under the age of five years, around 99% of the targeted population, were vaccinated/immunised throughout Sudan.
- Mass immunisation campaigns, such as the polio immunisation campaign in Malawi, which increased the number of immunised children from 85% in 2003 to 88% in 2007.
- Any other valid point. (Be aware that this is not a complete list. You may think of other possible ideas and examples yourself.)

What you should know…

UNICEF (United Nations Children's Fund)

UNICEF is the world's leading organisation focusing on children and children's rights, with a presence in more than 190 countries and territories. Some areas of its work include:

- Emergencies: Providing life-saving assistance to children affected by disasters. Since the December of 2004 tsunami that struck Indonesia, UNICEF has helped build nearly 350 new child-friendly and earthquake-resistant schools, benefiting many thousands of children.
- Health: In 2008, UNICEF supplied vaccines against killer disease for more than 56 per cent of the world's children and delivered over 19 million mosquito nets.
- Education: UNICEF supports governments and communities to build schools, train teachers and provide textbooks so that every child can get an education.
- Protection: 150 million children are currently involved in child labour. UNICEF works with families to address the underlying issues that force children into work, and provide training and rehabilitation for children who have been living on the streets or working.

Chapter 7 International Relations

What you should know…

FAO (Food and Agriculture Organization) www.fao.org

FAO specialises in raising levels of nutrition and working on methods to improve the supply from farmers. Initiatives have included:

- FAO helps governments train people to improve crop yield, quality of food and nutrition. It also provides hygiene advice. In 2009 FAO produced a manual about good hygiene practices regarding street food in Africa.

- Researching and developing farming methods. A research project was carried out between 1992–2006 in Kenya where a farm used improved technology to manage sustainability of crops and improve their community.

- Providing irrigation schemes, fertilising instructions and enhancing fisheries, forestry and cattle farming. In Ethiopia a four-year project was established in 2004, in conjunction with the Ethiopian and Italian governments at a cost of $3 000 000 to improve irrigation and water supplies to farming workers and associated beneficiaries. One such group were the 2000 farm households who benefited from irrigation, drainage and water management.

- Supplying experts, advisers and educators, such as technical advisers to forestry.

- Any other valid point. (Be aware that this is not a complete list. You may think of other possible ideas and examples yourself.)

What you should know…

WFP (World Food Programme)

WFP is the world's largest humanitarian agency, fighting hunger worldwide. It is part of the UN system, but is funded voluntarily. In 2010, WFP's aim is to reach more than 90 million people in 73 countries with food assistance. WFP also aims to do the following:

www.wfp.org

- Save lives and protect livelihoods in emergencies. WFP sends food assistance to these areas, saving the lives of victims of war, civil fighting and natural disasters. For example, in Somalia, where civil unrest is a major problem, WFP is aiming to feed 3·3 million people – or half of the population over the month of April 2010.

- WFP helps people prepare for emergencies. For example, in Kenya, WFP has tripled its 2009 assistance to help nearly four million people struggling with high food prices and food shortages after four consecutive failed harvests due to drought.

- WFP helps people rebuild their lives after emergencies. Following the genocide of the 1990s in Rwanda, WFP has helped 300 000 primary school children receive a hot lunch in 300 schools situated in the most food-insecure parts of the country. This allows the children to have at least one proper meal each day.

- WFP aims to reduce hunger and under nutrition. In Chad, WFP provides food assistance through general food distributions, supplementary feeding for children under five, as well as for pregnant women and those bringing up newborn babies.

continued

Standard Grade Modern Studies

What you should know – continued

- WFP tries to strengthen the capacity of countries to reduce hunger. In Ethiopia, WFP has set up a Purchase for Progress scheme. This is where WFP buys food from local farmers and markets to give to the people in need. This way, the food is grown in the country and helps local farmers make money. The Bill Gates Foundation is one of the groups which help fund this scheme.

- Any other valid point. (Be aware that this is not a complete list. You may think of other possible ideas and examples yourself.)

What you should know…

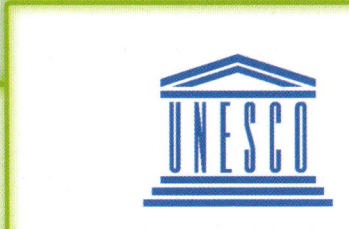

UNESCO (United Nations Educational, Scientific and Cultural Organization)

Education is one of UNESCO's principal activities. The others are science, culture and communication. Since 1945, the Organization has worked to help build sustainable, just societies that value knowledge, promote peace and celebrate diversity through providing Education for All. Through its links with education ministries and other partners in 193 countries, UNESCO:

www.unesco.org

- Promotes education for all men, women and children as a basic human right.
- Sends experts to help countries improve their education systems.
- Carries out and publishes research on the state of education globally.
- Advocates for more investment in education.
- Facilitates policy dialogue, knowledge sharing and capacity-building to improve the quality of education.

What you should know…

ILO (International Labour Organization)

The ILO tries to improve working conditions. In African countries, wages are often low, working conditions are poor and unsafe and many children are forced to work. The ILO works in many ways:

- Improving work conditions and health and safety. One such example to highlight this goal is the annual Occupational Safety and Health month. This is held in a different country each year, such as Cameroon or Nigeria.

- Helping those children who are forced to work long hours in poor conditions. In Tanzania hundreds of child workers have been taken out of domestic service jobs by the ILO and returned to their families and schools.

- Offering help to those who run businesses and factories.

- Any other valid point. (Be aware that this is not a complete list. You may think of other possible ideas and examples yourself.)

www.ilo.org

Look out for

A good knowledge of **two** agencies is sufficient for both General and Credit levels.

Chapter 7 International Relations

General question (2002 Q4a)

> United Nations aid **meets the needs** of developing countries in Africa in a number of different ways.

Describe **two** ways in which United Nations aid **meets the needs** of developing countries in Africa.

(KU, 4 marks)

A good answer will take points and examples from the information and develop them.

You should give detailed descriptions of the types of aid given. You must describe **two** ways the United Nations meets the needs of developing countries **and** give examples.

This information directs you to some of the points you could use in your answer. For example, one type of United Nations aid is provided by Unicef. The aid which Unicef could give is to provide emergency relief to children after a disaster. For example, in Sudan, following civil war and mass starvation and evacuation of homes, a measles epidemic broke out. Unicef responded by immunising 15 000 children in one town.

General answer

You could use the examples of the World Health Organisation and Unicef.

One way in which United Nations aid helps meet the needs of developing countries in Africa is through the World Health Organisation (WHO). The WHO tries to help meet the medical needs of people. One way they try to do this is through delivering improved health services in developing countries. For example in 2008, WHO helped establish Sudan's first mental health clinic to help treat Sudanese people who suffered from depression following the civil war in Sudan which came to an end in 2005.

A second way in which the United Nations helps meet the needs of developing African countries is through Unicef. Unicef mainly focuses on improving the lives of young children through improving education, providing suitable health care and by helping to give a safe home. One way Unicef could help meet needs is carrying out immunisation programmes in towns and villages. For example, Unicef recently carried out a malaria programme in Zambia.

! Look out for
Remember for General answers you must PEE!

Make sure you remember the different colours for PEE!

! Look out for
Make sure you clearly show understanding of the question and the examples you are giving in your answer.

Credit question

You may be asked a Credit question based on the same theme (types of aid or aid agencies), as was asked at General level. However, at Credit level it will be more specific. The following question requires explicit examples to **prove** that the UN has helped meet the needs of some African countries.

Standard Grade Modern Studies

Credit question (2005 Q4b)

> The aid policies of the United Nations have helped meet the needs of some African countries.

Describe, **in detail**, the ways in which the aid policies of the United Nations have helped meet the needs of some African countries.

(KU, 4 marks)

You should give **detailed** descriptions of the types of aid that UN agencies such as Unicef provide. You must also give examples you have studied to show **how** these agencies have helped to meet the needs of African countries.

Credit answer

The United Nations has many aims. A specific aim is encouraging social and economic progress. One way the UN helps meet the needs of people is through their specialised aid agencies. One such agency is Unicef. Unicef mainly focuses on improving the life of young children through improving universal education, providing suitable health care and helping to ensure a safe home. Unicef tries to develop education by establishing schools, encouraging young children to return to education and by helping to educate parents. For example in Gambia there are 65 Mother's Clubs which aim to help educate young mothers and children about education and to overcome the resistance to girls receiving an education. Initiatives such as these helped primary school enrolment in developing countries in 2006 reach 88% on average, up from 83% in 2000. By giving this opportunity, Unicef is developing social progress among women and children.

A further way the United Nations has helped meet the needs of some African countries is through the World Health Organisation. The WHO aims to help meet medical needs by promoting good health and developing medical facilities and access to them. One way they have succeeded is by providing polio vaccinations to almost every child aged under five years in Sudan. This followed the civil war and humanitarian crisis in the country. Due to the success of this programme, it can be argued that the United Nations is helping to meet the needs of some African countries.

Look out for

Remember at Credit level you must PEER! Point, Explain, Example, Relate.

Tied aid

What you should know…

Sometimes aid can be referred to as **TIED AID**. This term is used when conditions are attached to the aid, hence the term Tied. This, for example, is when a donor country gives aid, such as farming aid, but there will be conditions to the aid. It could be that the receiving country has to spend the farming aid in the country that gives it. For example the UK may insist that Mozambique buy tractors from UK suppliers with the aid funding.

Chapter 7 International Relations

Political, social and economic factors

What you should know...

> The concept being assessed is **power.** *You should know that developed countries hold power over developing countries.*

An area you can be questioned on at Credit level is 'the political, social and economic factors developed countries consider before giving aid to developing countries.' This area has never been examined before at General level. **However** this does not mean it won't be at some stage.

Definition of developed and developing nations

Developed nation: The term **developed nation** is used to describe countries that have a high level of development. These nations have good social and economic factors, based on high living standards, a good health service, low rates of infant death, and high levels of economic development. Countries such as Canada, the UK and the USA are examples of developed nations.

Developing nation: The term **developing nation** is used to describe a nation with a low level of material well being. They have a low level of development. These nations have social and economic problems, such as low living standards, low levels of healthcare, high illiteracy levels and a high level of infant death. Countries such as Ethiopia, Somalia and Rwanda are examples of developing nations.

There are many factors that developed nations consider before they give aid to developing nations.

They can be identified as: **Political**

 Social

 Economic

Blue = High Income Nations
Green = Upper/Middle Income Nations
Purple = Middle/Lower Income Nations
Red = Low Income Nations

- Political factors are issues such as: wars which prevent people from using the land to grow crops (can the government ensure the safe passage of aid?); corrupt governments or dictatorships (does the government support enemies of the UK, for example?); geographical location; giving aid may help the donor nation's worldwide image.

- Social factors are issues such as: education levels; literacy levels; traditions which affect production, such as working times; unemployment rates; health problems/disease; attitudes towards women and children.

- Economic factors are issues such as: high debt levels (does the developing nation owe more than it makes from exports?); wage levels in the country; the products countries produce to generate money (do they rely on a single product?).

Developed nations can also use their economic power to influence smaller nations. They may give aid to nations with good natural resources, such as oil or gas. They may insist that developing countries change the products (cash crops) they produce for sale in developed markets. They can also use their influence in organisations such as the UN to encourage trade barriers (sanctions).

Standard Grade Modern Studies

Credit question (2003 Q4a)

> Political factors are taken into account by developed countries before deciding which countries in Africa should receive aid.
>
> Describe, **in detail**, the political factors which are taken into account by developed countries before deciding which countries in Africa should receive aid.
>
> (KU, 4 marks)

Look out for

Make very sure you answer the specific detail of a question like this. Only describe **Political** factors. If you include factors such as debt levels or health issues you will not receive the marks, as these are economic and social issues.

Credit answer

A typical Credit answer to this question could be:

> One political factor to be taken into account by a developed nation before deciding which countries in Africa should receive aid is whether or not the developing country is a democracy. Countries in the developed world, such as the UK, are more likely to give aid to a country with a similar political structure, where political parties and the public are allowed free speech and the public can vote for whoever they wish as their representative in Parliament. If a similar system is in place in a developing nation, the UK is more likely to offer aid. For example, a developing nation such as South Africa which has free elections for the adult population, as well as a high number of participating political parties is more likely to receive aid as it has a political system liked by the UK. This shows that if a country has a political system similar to that of the donor country it is much more likely to receive aid as they will get along politically.
>
> A further political factor which may be considered before giving aid is the geographical location of a country. The USA may give aid to a country which they can use as a military base if they are in conflict with a neighbouring country. This means that they will use the country to train troops in conditions of extreme/hot weather, to base their equipment and forces there, near to the country they are in conflict with. This will benefit the developed country as it will have easier access to the conflict. In return it will provide aid to the developing nation they are based in. For example the USA was until recently involved in a conflict with Somalia. In order to be based and train near to this country, the American forces could have based themselves in Ethiopia, which shares a border with Somalia. Therefore if there is a benefit for the developed country it is more likely to give aid, as they can use the likes of Ethiopia when they need their help.

In order to answer this question you must understand the various political factors concerned. You must be able to give relevant examples you have studied.

Look out for

Remember to construct your answer to this type of question in the same way as shown here. The content will change depending on whether the question asks for political, social or economic factors. BUT the method you use to answer the question should not change.

Chapter 7 International Relations

Credit question (2005 Q4a)

> Wealthy countries have had economic power over African countries in recent years.

Describe, **in detail**, the ways in which wealthy countries from outside Africa have used their **economic power** in their relations with less well-off African countries in recent years.

(KU, 4 marks)

Look out for

Remember to focus on what the question asks. The question asks about **ECONOMIC** power, so that is what you focus your answer on.

Credit answer

An example of **one** paragraph is given below. This is not a complete answer.

> Nations such as the USA can use their economic power over less well-off African countries in a number of ways. One way they can use this economic power is through trade barriers. A trade barrier is an agreement set up to stop countries trading their goods to other countries, with the result that the country cannot sell goods to make money, nor can they buy the goods they may need to provide for the people of their country. Trade barriers make it very difficult for countries to function correctly and they give a great deal of power to other countries. An example of this is the United Nations, with USA as a member, placing a trade barrier on Zimbabwe to try to force President Mugabe to change the way he runs the country. This barrier stopped Zimbabwe selling goods to other countries, helping contribute to their 94% unemployment rate in January 2009 and it prevented Zimbabwean people getting the goods they needed. This shows that powerful countries like the USA have a great deal of influence, as they can impose trade barriers with countries such as Zimbabwe.

Only one detailed way has been provided for this question. Try to produce a second reason yourself!

Look out for

Remember to base it on the PEER technique used for the first argument.

Does aid meet the needs of those who require it?

What you should know…

> The concept being assessed is **need**. Does the aid meet the needs of the people who require it?

An area you can be questioned on at Credit level is 'does aid meet the needs of those who require it the most?'

This area has not been examined at General level. **However** this does not mean it won't be at some stage.

We have provided a recap summary of the main issues. Afterwards there is a sample Credit question and answer.

Summary

There now comes quite a hard question to think through! Because Africa is such a large continent and some of its countries have so many problems, it can be very difficult to ensure aid helps the people who need it the most.

So why do so many people not receive the aid help they need?

- Sometimes the aid sent is not what is most appropriate. Will sending hi-tech field ploughs help a farmer if he does not have the training to work the machinery?
- If literacy levels are poor, people may not be able to read the instructions. For example, sending medical supplies will not benefit some people if they cannot read the dosage.
- Developed nations may decide to send aid in a large scale form. They may provide the material to build airports or bridges. However most of the country's people will not need these. Rather, they will need village clinics and schools.
- Aid may be tied. A developed country may insist aid is spent on weapons or vehicle parts. Again this will not benefit most people.
- Governments may be corrupt and prevent the distribution of aid to the country's towns and villages through the use of the army.
- Any other valid point. (Be aware that this is not a complete list. You may think of other possible ideas and examples yourself.)

Credit question (2003 Q4a)

> Some people feel that the aid which is given to African countries does not meet the needs of the majority of the people.
>
> Explain, **in detail**, why some people in African countries feel that the aid which is given to African countries does not meet the needs of the majority of the people.
>
> (KU, 4 marks)

Look out for

Remember to always think which concept the question relates to. Is it Power or Need?

Chapter 7 International Relations

Credit answer

An example of **one** paragraph is given below. This is not a complete answer.

> One reason why some people feel the aid given to African countries does not meet the needs of the majority of people is that the aid sent is on a large scale. This may only benefit one or two areas of a country. This means it may not be specific to what the people feel they need. They may need many small scale projects which help cities, towns and villages throughout the country. An example of this could be that many developed nations, through an organisation such as the EU, may decide to help build a large scale bridge connecting two areas in a country such as Zambia. Although this will help some people travel and transport goods, it will not help the rest of the country. The population may feel the aid would be better given to providing clean water, improved diets and health education for the citizens of Zambia. This may then help improve their average life expectancy rate which is approximately 38 years of age. Therefore it may be, because of certain initiatives like large scale projects, the aid that is needed doesn't get to the people of the country. As is clear in the case of Zambia, a more pressing issue than a bridge requiring aid is the average life expectancy.

Issues that prevent needs being met

What you should know…

> The concept being assessed is **equality**. *The life differences between groups of people.*

An area you can be questioned on at General and Credit levels is 'the reasons why certain issues prevent African governments from meeting the needs of their people.'

We have provided a recap summary of the main reasons. Afterwards there are sample General and Credit questions and answers.

Summary

One of the major problems African governments can encounter when attempting to meet the needs of their people, is outside factors. Factors such as:

- AIDS/HIV: Many African nations suffer enormous problems with this disease. It results in severe illness and death, meaning people cannot work, children become orphaned and have to look after siblings, which prevents them attending school. Also governments have to redirect money away from education, housing and food to pay for treatment of AIDS/HIV.

An estimated 22 million adults and children were living with HIV in Sub-Saharan Africa at the end of 2008.

continued

Standard Grade Modern Studies

What you should know – continued

During that year, an estimated 1·5 million Africans died from AIDS. This has left behind 11·6 million orphaned children.

In 2007 in Cameroon 540 000 people suffered from HIV/AIDS. This is 5·1% of the population. Of this number 39 000 died. There is currently thought to be 300 000 AIDS orphans living in Cameroon.

- WAR: Wars (both external and civil) greatly affect Sub-Saharan Africa. Roads for transport and fields for farming get destroyed. People are killed or forced to flee their homes and towns. This means they cannot work. Aid and goods are seized by the armies to fuel their soldiers. Many children are captured by armies such as the Revolutionary United Front in Sierra Leone to become child soldiers or workers. It is thought that 1000 people are dying every day from war-related causes, including disease, hunger and violence in the Democratic Republic of Congo.

- DROUGHT: This is a major factor as people need water to survive. The main problem is not lack of rainfall. The average rainfall in London is 24 inches per year and in Addis Ababa, the capital of Ethiopia, a country which has suffered severe drought, the average rainfall is 48 inches. Lack of proper drainage and sewage infrastructure is a big problem. This leads to rainwater being lost and disease and bacteria entering the water supply when fields flood and drains overflow. Because people have little choice they have to drink, cook, wash and work with this contaminated water. This causes diseases such as diarrhea and typhoid. Because of a lack of basic health care, people die from these diseases. This leads to problems such as no work force, orphans and people unable to farm land and grow crops for consumption and sale.

- Any other valid point. (Be aware that this is not a complete list. You may think of other possible ideas and examples yourself.) Look at these aid charity websites: www.savethechildren.org.uk, www.oxfam.org.uk, www.sciaf.org.uk, www.wateraid.org, www.unaids.org.

General question (2009 Q4a)

Problems faced by some African countries

War/Conflict	Debt	HIV/AIDS	Unsafe water

Choose **two** of the problems shown above.
Describe how each of the problems you have chosen affects some African countries.

(KU, 4 marks)

*For full marks you must answer on **two** of the problems.*

Try to answer this question using PEE.

Chapter 7 International Relations

Credit question (2008 Q4a)

| HIV/AIDS on the increase in large parts of Africa | Civil wars rage on in parts of Africa | Prices fall on a number of raw materials produced in some African countries |

Choose **one** issue from the boxes above.
Explain, **in detail**, why your chosen issue may prevent some African governments **meeting the needs** of their people.

(KU, 4 marks)

Look out for

The question asks you to choose **one** issue. **Do not** answer about them all! This is a common mistake!

Look out for

You will be asked to explain two issues for 4 marks at General level and one issue for 4 marks at Credit level.

Credit answer

An example of **one** paragraph is given below. This is not a complete answer.

Many governments in Africa are prevented from meeting the needs of their people due to HIV/AIDS for a number of reasons. One reason is due to the huge death toll caused by the disease. Thousands die throughout countries in Sub Saharan Africa each year. This makes it hard for the government to earn money through the products that the country produces, as there is a lack of skilled workers because of the disease. Because of the death toll there is no continuity in work and production. This means work places and industries must keep finding new workers. For example in Botswana 24% of the population are infected by HIV/AIDS. This makes it very difficult for them to work and provide for their families. The country's main industries are diamonds and copper, which require skilled workers. With some 300 000 people living with the disease it is difficult to have these continued skills. Therefore this shows that due to the high disease rates in countries such as Botswana, it is very difficult to sustain workers in the main industries. This means the government does not gain the money required to provide for the country.

Try to complete the answer using the PEER method.

Standard Grade Modern Studies

Alliances

There are four key areas you can be questioned on at General and/or Credit level with regards to alliances in International Relations:

- The reasons why countries wish to join the European Union.
- The reasons why countries wish to have membership of NATO.
- The actions which alliances take to combat the threat to their security and the threat of terrorism.
- The actions taken by governments to protect their country from threats to their security.

Look out for

In previous years the International Relations topics would alternate. If Politics of Aid appeared in the 2002 General paper, it would mean that Alliances would be in the Credit paper. Added to this, it would be a guarantee that the following year the sequence would be alternated, i.e. Politics of Aid would appear at Credit level and Alliances would be at General level. **This is no longer the case!** This system stopped in the 2007 Modern Studies examination. Now the two topic areas are mixed in together. The General and Credit papers will have both Politics of Aid and Alliances questions. This means you must know both areas to a good standard, particularly at KU.

The reasons why countries want to join the European Union

What you should know…

> The concept being assessed is **need.** *The needs of a country being met to benefit its people.*

An area you can be questioned on at both General and Credit levels is 'the reasons why countries have joined or want to join the European Union'.

We have provided below a recap summary to remind you of the main reasons. Afterwards there is a series of example General and Credit KU questions and sample answers.

continued

103

Chapter 7 International Relations

What you should know – continued

Summary

- Countries benefit from trade deals with other countries. There are relaxed trade barriers between member states. This allows goods to be bought and sold much more easily. It brings great wealth to a country.

- New member states may have lower wage costs, therefore production costs of goods is reduced, meaning these goods can be bought for a cheaper price by EU citizens.

- Countries can benefit from the Euro currency, as it allows businesses to trade with each other in the same currency. This encourages trade, without exchange rates and charges.

- Membership allows freedom of travel and work for citizens of member states. This opens education and employment opportunities.

- Aid is available to member states. Funding is available to all nations, particularly poorer nations, such as Latvia. Programmes such as infrastructure and tourism can be funded by EU aid. For example regional aid was given for investment in the Falkirk Wheel tourist project.

- Countries with a strong fishing industry can benefit from membership of the Common Fisheries Policy. This ensures a fair price for products, a quota system to protect future fish stocks and a safer fishing environment with strict safety guidelines.

- The European Defence Force is in place to help protect member nations and their citizens. Members work cooperatively to provide manpower and equipment in times of conflict. For example, in 2004, the defence force took over peacekeeping duties in Bosnia-Herzegovina.

- Any other valid point. (Be aware that this is not a complete list. You may think of other possible ideas and examples yourself. Look at www.europa.eu.)

General question (2005 Q4b)

> Many countries have joined the European Union recently.
>
> Give **two** reasons to explain why many countries have joined the European Union recently.
>
> (KU, 4 marks)

Standard Grade Modern Studies

General question (2008 Q4c)

10 things you should know about the European Union (EU)
1. The European Union is a group of countries whose governments work together.
2. It's a bit like a club. To join you have to agree to follow the rules and in return you get certain benefits.
3. Each country has to pay money to be a member. They mostly do this through taxes.
4. The Single European Market has made trade between countries much easier.
5. There are 5 countries wishing to join at the moment, including Bulgaria, Romania and Turkey.
6. 43% of all spending by the EU goes on Agriculture, Fisheries and helping the environment.
7. The EU has banned animal testing for cosmetics.
8. EU regional aid has raised living standards in poorer parts of Europe.
9. In 2002, 8 out of 10 EU citizens said they were fairly or very satisfied with living in the EU.
10. The EU has helped over 2 million young people study in another country.

Countries still wish to join the European Union.

Give **two** reasons why countries still wish to join the European Union.
To answer this question, you may wish to use the information above.

(KU, 4 marks)

!**Look out for**

The information box called '10 things you should know...' has a lot of information to help you answer the question. **However** it was felt by the SQA that it was perhaps too much information and G/C pupils found it a little confusing. Therefore the SQA has decided that questions in the future on any syllabus area **will not** include this style of prompt to help you.

General question (2009 Q4c)

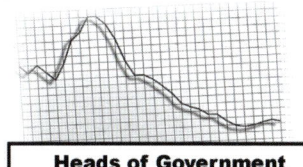

INCREASED SALES TO EUROPE | NEW ROAD BRIDGE | FERRY TERMINAL Gateway to Europe | Heads of Government Meeting over Banking Crisis

Countries like the UK can benefit from being members of the European Union.

Give **two** ways in which a country like the UK can benefit from being a member of the European Union. For **one** of the ways, describe how a country like the UK could benefit.
To answer this question, you may wish to use the drawings above.

(KU, 4 marks)

Chapter 7 International Relations

These three questions are very similar in style. The first and second questions are almost identical in their wording. They deal with the reasons why countries **want to be members** of the EU. The first question is about why countries have joined, the second about why countries want to join. They are both about the advantages of membership. Although the third question may look different, it too is very similar. It focuses on the benefits of membership. This is exactly the same as the first and second questions. The only difference is that it has an additional question part. However, this is merely prompting you to provide a UK example.

Let's now try a sample answer to this question area.

General answer (2005 Q4b)

One reason why many countries have joined the European Union recently is because the country and its businesses benefit from trade deals with other member nations. This means that businesses in different countries can buy goods from and sell goods to each other much more easily, without complication and barriers. Businesses in member nations will no longer have tax to pay when buying products from EU countries. This means that they can pay a lesser price for the product, meaning the customer can buy the product at a cheaper price. For example, the Scottish car dealer Arnold Clark, which employs thousands of people throughout the United Kingdom, will not have trade barriers in place when they buy Renault cars from France to sell in this country. This means they can pay less and sell to customers for less than they would have if the UK was not an EU member.

A second reason why countries have joined the EU is because of the aid which is available to member nations. The EU Regional Aid fund helps pay for projects in EU areas in order to improve the economic life of the area. This helps as it brings jobs and visitors to the area. Only members of the EU can apply for this aid. For example the Rosyth ferry terminal on the east coast of Scotland received EU aid money in the early part of 2000 to improve the ferry ports and allow people and goods to travel more easily for business and holidays. Rosyth is a main route by sea from Scotland to countries such as the Netherlands and other parts of Europe. This project helped bring more business and tourists to Scotland and the UK.

You should see very clearly where this question has been answered, using PEE. There is a clear reason why countries have joined the EU. This is in black. There is a clear explanation of why this is a good reason for joining. This section is in green. And, finally, an example is given to prove the explanation of the reason. This section is in violet.

Using this very same system, answer the 2008 and 2009 questions yourself.

Credit question (2004 Q4b)

> Countries joining the European Union (EU) recently have done so for economic reasons.

Explain, **in detail**, the economic reasons for countries joining the European Union (EU).

(KU, 4 marks)

106

Standard Grade Modern Studies

Credit question (2007 Q4a)

> The policies of the European Union (EU) try to meet the **needs** of member countries and their citizens.

Choose **two** of the following policies.
- Single European Currency (Euro)
- Enlarged Membership
- Common Fisheries Policy
- Aid to the Regions
- European Defence Force
- Common Agricultural Policy

For **each** policy, describe, **in detail**, the ways in which it tries to meet the **needs** of member countries and their citizens.

In your answer, you **must** use recent examples you have studied.

(KU, 8 marks)

!**Look out for**

Key words in a question instruction, such as **recent examples**.

!**Look out for**

This is a far more common style of question!

The two Credit questions both deal with the benefits of joining the European Union. The first question looks at the **economic benefits** of EU membership. The second question is more focused. For this you need to have a good level of knowledge and understanding of EU policies and how they benefit member countries.

Credit answer (2007 Q4a)

An example of **one** paragraph is given below. This is not a complete answer.

> The European Union has many policies aimed at meeting the needs of member countries and its citizens. One policy which aims to do this is the Single European Currency, the Euro. The policy of the Euro tries to meet the needs of members by allowing businesses to trade with each other using the same currency of money. This encourages trade by simplifying business deals. It also saves businesses money as there is no commission on money being exchanged from one currency to another. This allows companies to grow and keep costs low, allowing customers to buy products at lower prices. For example, the Euro encouraging a strong market allows companies such as Ryanair, the Irish aeroplane company, to trade with suppliers, such as BMW engines, of Germany. The existence of the Euro ensures exchange and tax barriers are not in place, meaning costs can be kept as low as possible for customers, which means their needs are met, as they retain more of their money.

Use the PEER method to answer the rest of this question.

Chapter 7 International Relations

The reasons why countries wish to be members of NATO

What you should know…

> The concepts being assessed are **need and power.**
> *The needs of countries and the power it gives them.*

An area you can be questioned on at General and Credit levels is 'the reasons why countries wish to join the North Atlantic Treaty Organisation (NATO)'.

We have provided below a recap summary to remind you of the main reasons. Afterwards there is an example General KU question and sample answer.

Summary

- Membership of NATO gives added protection to a country from possible enemies.
- If any NATO member country is attacked the other 27 member countries will support it in the hostilities. This gives major military, economic and resource support.
- Many newer members are smaller, less powerful countries, such as Latvia and Lithuania. Membership gives them much more security from threats.
- NATO helps stabilise newer countries such as the Czech Republic and Slovakia. NATO is experienced in helping to establish democracy in member countries. This helps newer democracies.
- NATO helps protect countries from the threats of terrorism in the world. Any member nation attacked by terrorists is supported by other members.
- NATO has installed anti-terror programmes through out the world, such as Operation Active Endeavour, which patrols the Mediterranean Sea, in order to help deter terrorist activity.
- NATO helps coordinate anti-terror operations throughout the world from its headquarters in Brussels, Belgium.
- Any other valid point. (Be aware that this is not a complete list. You may think of other possible ideas and examples yourself. Look at www.nato.int.)

NATO peacekeeping soldiers

Standard Grade Modern Studies

General question (2003 Q4a)

> There are a number of countries in Europe wanting to join NATO.
>
> Give **two** reasons why a number of countries want to join NATO.
>
> (KU, 4 marks)

Questions which ask, 'why are countries members of NATO?', or 'what are the benefits of NATO membership?', or even 'why do a number of countries want to join NATO?' are asking you the exact same thing. You are being asked to give the advantages/benefits/plus points of a country being part of NATO.

General answer

One reason why a number of countries want to join NATO is because of the added security protection it gives. NATO is made up of 28 member nations. They help add to the strength of military, financial and weapon power that NATO has. If a member country comes under attack from an enemy nation, they will be supported by all the NATO members. This gives an enormous amount of help in a war situation. For example, as a member of NATO, Estonia, with a population of 1·3 million people, is limited in the military power it has. However if it was attacked by an aggressor and threatened by war, the other NATO members would support them. This means that countries like the USA, with armed forces of almost 1·5 million, could help defend and fight alongside Estonia.

A second reason why a country may wish to join NATO is due to the role NATO plays in countering terrorism in the world. NATO has an enormous number of military personnel at its disposal. It uses this to set up anti-terror operations in different areas of the world. This helps to defend member countries from the threat of terrorism. For example Operation Active Endeavour was established in late 2001 after the 9/11 terror attack. This programme allows warships to patrol the Mediterranean Sea searching for terrorist and criminal activities. This helps protect NATO members such as Spain, which has a coastline on the Mediterranean Sea, from the threat of terrorism.

Credit questions

Credit question 2002, Q4b focuses on Eastern European countries joining NATO. The questions have started to move away from this area, as uncertainty in the former Soviet Union has been replaced as an area of focus by international security. Questions now focus much more on the measures taken by countries and organisations to protect themselves from the threat to security and the threat of terrorism. We will look at this area in more detail in the following sections.

Chapter 7 International Relations

The actions taken by alliances to combat the threat to security and the threat of terror

What you should know…

> The concept being assessed is **power.** *The power of alliances to protect security.*

An area you can be questioned on at General and Credit levels is 'the methods used by alliances such as the UN and/or NATO to combat terrorism and the threat to international security'.

Below is a summary recap of this area. Although questions relating to security and terrorism **do not focus specifically on alliances**, it is very worthwhile knowing the methods NATO/UN use in relation to other countries.

Summary

- NATO established Operation Active Endeavour following 9/11. It was established to protect the Mediterranean Sea area from terrorist and criminal activities. It gave NATO warships the power to board and seize ships which were thought to be suspicious. So far, over 150 suspect vessels have been boarded.

- Italy and the NATO Undersea Research Centre protect harbours and ships from underwater threats. They use sensor nets, detectors and unmanned underwater vehicles to detect illegal activity.

- NATO, along with Bulgaria and Greece, has been at the forefront of protecting helicopters from rocket grenades. Research has gone into detecting these rockets, giving greater protection to aircraft and passengers.

- NATO has a Counter Terrorism Technology Coordinator and has set up a Counter-Terrorism Technology Unit to oversee efforts to protect and support nations.

- NATO established AWAC (Airborne Warning and Control System) planes. They monitor airspace with superior radar in order to detect terrorist attacks. They provide protection at events such as the 2006 World Cup and President Obama's visit to Germany in June 2009.

- NATO troops are currently serving in Afghanistan in the fight against terror.

- NATO troops, including US personnel, are working to stabilise the democratic process in Iraq.

- The United Nations counters terrorism through many of its agencies. The International Civil Aviation Organisation (ICAO) is the UN body responsible for developing aviation security. It examines airline and airport security systems. The Office for Drug Control and Crime Prevention (ODCCP) has a special database on terrorism. It monitors patterns of terror and investigates the links between terror and drug sales. Often terrorism is paid for by crime and drugs. (Look at www.un.org.)

continued

Standard Grade Modern Studies

What you should know – continued

- The United Nations Assistance Mission in Afghanistan (UNAMA), is in place to support the elections of August 2009. UNAMA also helps the government carry out democracy, fight corruption and has a key role to play in safely delivering humanitarian aid to civilians in Afghanistan.
- The UK has been, until recently, involved in the war in Iraq, as part of the coalition force.
- The UK has been part of the war on terrorism in Afghanistan. UK forces have hunted for Osama Bin Laden.
- Any other valid point. (Be aware that this is not a complete list. You may think of other possible ideas and examples yourself.)

The actions taken by governments to protect security and combat terrorism

What you should know…

> The concept being assessed is **power.** *The powers countries have to protect themselves.*

An area you can be questioned on at General and Credit levels is 'the responses taken by countries to protect their security from the threat of terrorism'.

We have provided below a recap summary to remind you of the main reasons. Afterwards there is a series of example General and Credit KU questions and sample answers.

Summary

- International airports have altered security. There has been a reduction in hand luggage on board planes, armed police patrol airports, such as Glasgow International Airport and liquids over 100ml are not allowed through security checks.
- A Border Agency has been established to monitor movement over national borders.
- New buildings are now designed with security in mind. For example, the Scottish Parliament has concrete bollards in front of the building, with no vehicle access around it. Windows are also reinforced with six-inch thick glass.
- Litter bins have been removed from transport links, such as train stations. This reduces the risk of devices being planted.
- Many countries, such as the USA and the UK, joined the invasion of Afghanistan for the 'War on Terror'. This took place following 9/11.

continued

Chapter 7 International Relations

What you should know – continued

- Countries such as the USA have built missile defence systems to counter the threat of North Korea and Iran who have built new nuclear missiles.
- Russian diplomats have been banned from the UK following Russia's invasion of Georgia.
- Any other valid point. (Be aware that this is not a complete list. You may think of other possible ideas and examples yourself.)

General question (2005 Q4a)

> European Countries such as the UK have been involved in international conflicts in recent years.
>
> Describe **two** ways in which European countries such as the UK have been involved in international conflicts in recent years. In your answer, refer to examples that you have studied.
>
> (KU, 4 marks)

*This area of questioning has moved away from specific conflicts, such as Afghanistan, Iraq, etc., to looking more specifically at the methods countries such as the UK use to deter conflict/threats. You should therefore be aware of the subtle difference between this 2005 question and the more up-to-date focus on security threat and terrorism. **However** this **does not** mean Afghanistan and Iraq will not be examined in the future.*

Look out for!

Question focuses on *European* countries.

General answer

An example of **one** paragraph is given below. This is not a complete answer.

> *One way in which European countries such as the UK have been involved in international conflicts in recent years is through involvement in the war on terror. The UK sent forces to Afghanistan following the 9/11 terrorism attacks. UK forces were sent to fight Taliban forces, who were supporters of terrorism. For example, UK forces were given the task of finding Osama Bin Laden, who was thought to be behind the 9/11 terrorist attacks.*

Use the PEE method to complete this answer.

Credit question (2004 Q4a)

> European countries have taken security measures to protect themselves against threats such as international terrorism.
>
> Describe, **in detail**, some of the security measures taken by European countries to protect themselves against threats such as international terrorism.
>
> (KU, 4 marks)

Standard Grade Modern Studies

Credit question (2006 Q4a)

> In recent years some European countries and their allies have expanded their military actions beyond Europe.

Explain, **in detail**, the reasons why some European countries and their allies have expanded their military actions beyond Europe.
In answering this question, you must refer to:
- A description of some of these actions.
- The reasons why such actions were taken.

Your answer **must** refer to recent examples you have studied.

(KU, 8 marks)

*The key aspect of this question is ensuring you focus on **actions beyond Europe**. If you focus on actions in Europe, such as reacting to the war on terror in London, Glasgow and Madrid, for example, you will not gain the marks, as you have not correctly followed the question guidelines. This question requires you to focus on Iraq, Afghanistan, North Korea, etc.*

Credit question (2008 Q4b)

> European governments have taken actions to protect their populations from possible threats to their security.

Describe, **in detail**, some of the actions taken by European governments to protect their populations from possible threats to their security.

(KU, 4 marks)

'Threats to security' means exactly the same as 'threats of terrorism', i.e. possible threats of terrorism.

Credit question (2009 Q4a)

> A number of European countries have faced threats to their security. They have responded in different ways.

Describe, **in detail**:
- The threats these countries have faced.
- The ways in which they have responded to these threats.

(KU, 8 marks)

This 2009 question, if answering on international terrorism, is exactly the same as the 2008 question. The terrorism part of your answer could/should include very similar detail.

The 2009 question is worth twice as many marks as the 2008 question, however, as you are expected to have a deep understanding of the threats to security. (These are not asked for in 2008, the question only asks for actions taken.) You must focus on issues other than just terrorism, such as nuclear weapon threats, the threat of Russia to Georgia, etc.

113

Chapter 7 International Relations

! Look out for

Because this question guides you towards answering on two issues – the threats faced and the ways countries have responded – you should provide three relevant points in your answer, i.e. threat and a response is **one** relevant point. Therefore you would have to provide three threats and responses! The SQA marking guide advises a maximum of 3 marks per point, so you must provide three points for full marks. If you do not answer on either a threat or a response you can only receive 5 marks maximum.

Credit answer (2009 Q4a)

An example of **one** paragraph is given below. This is not a complete answer.

> In recent years European countries have faced many threats to their security. (1) One such threat has been the emergence of international terrorism. International terrorism has taken place in many areas of Europe such as the London transport bombings of July 2005 and the Glasgow Airport attack of June 2007. These attacks, in areas previously untouched by such acts, saw a change in the way security was carried out. (2) The UK Government has ensured that all airports now have much tighter security in place for passengers. Hand luggage is strictly controlled, with no dangerous objects, or liquids over 100ml, to be taken on board by hand. Passengers may not take sharp objects such as razor blades in their hand luggage. This shows that countries such as the UK have taken a serious approach to terrorist threats.

Number 1 = The threats the country has faced. Number 2 = The ways in which they have responded to these threats.

Complete the rest of this answer using the PEER method.

! Look out for

You can now download video clips and relevant programmes to help you absorb up-to-date details.

www.bbc.co.uk/iplayer
www.youtube.co.uk
www.channel4.com/4od
www.stv.tv

If you have missed a programme and you don't have internet access, why not contact the television station, and ask for them to send you a copy of the programme?

Enquiry Skills — Chapter 8

In this chapter, we will focus on Enquiry Skills (ES). Enquiry Skills is a key part of your Modern Studies course and examination. ES contributes 60% of the marks in the examination.

When answering ES questions you **MUST**:

- Read the question first of all before you read the sources. This gives you a better idea of what you are looking for in the sources.
- Be very aware of the number of marks available. Approach ES questions the same way as KU questions. For 4 marks, provide two answer parts, for 8 marks, provide four answer parts, etc.
- Never include material in your answer which is not from the source. The answer must be entirely based on source information. Do not give personal opinions or background knowledge. This will not receive any marks and will cost you valuable time.
- You must provide answers from all sources. If you do not use all sources in your answer, you cannot gain full marks.

Let's focus on the various types of ES questions, as detailed in Chapter 2. We will work through each one and look at appropriate answers.

We will begin with the ES General question types.

General Enquiry Skills

Differences

General question (2008 Q1b)

Sources 1 and 2 give different views about **representation in the House of Commons**.

Source 1

VIEW OF MALCOLM BROWN

There are about 5 million members of ethnic minority groups in Britain. The number of MPs from such ethnic groups rose slightly in 2005.

We do not need special arrangements to attract more women into Parliament. After the 2005 General Election, the number of women in the House of Commons rose to a historic high. 128 female MPs were elected. This shows that women are now well represented in the UK.

This was election win number three for Prime Minister Blair and his party.

Source 2

VIEW OF JANE RENNIE

The 2005 election was the third win in a row for Tony Blair and the Labour Party.

With 128 MPs, there are more women in the House of Commons than ever before. However, with less than 20% of the total, women in the UK are still poorly represented when compared to other European countries. We must find new ways to encourage more women to become MPs.

The number of representatives from Britain's 5 million or so ethnic minority population has increased a little from 13 to 15 MPs.

Write down **two** differences between these views.

You **must** only use the information from the sources above.

(ES, 4 marks)

*Automatically you should be looking for things that are **different** between the two sources. The trick is to look for a difference about the same issue between source 1 and source 2. In total you will have one issue that is different between source 1 and source 2 **AND** a second issue that is different between the sources. This will give you your **two** differences.*

Chapter 8 Enquiry Skills

General answer

One difference about representation in the House of Commons is that source 1 states that *'We do not need special arrangements to attract more women into Parliament'*. However source 2 states that *'We must find new ways to encourage more women to become MPs'*. These are clearly different views about women becoming MPs.

A second difference between the views is that source 1 argues 'After the 2005 General Election, the number of women in the House of Commons reached a historic high of 128 MPs. *This shows that women are now well represented in the UK'*. However source 2 is different as it states, 'However with less than 20% of the total, *women in the UK are still poorly represented when compared to other European countries'*. This shows different views about how well women are represented.

> You should see the differences between the views. They have been highlighted in **red** for you.

Look out for

The titles of sources. They can give hints to the content of the source.

*Try other **Differences** questions from the Bright Red General Past Papers for Modern Studies.*

Option choice

General question (2007 Q2a)

Information on Millie Smith

Millie Smith is 72 years old and lives in a 4 bedroomed house which is too big for her. Her husband died recently and she feels lonely. She has always enjoyed having a garden. She has recently had a hip operation and finds it more difficult to move about or do the housework. Millie is starting to feel the cold more and more.

Millie wants to buy another home. She has seen the two houses below but is not sure whether **House A or House B** would **better meet her** needs.

House A – Ground Floor Flat

A ground floor, 2 bedroomed flat in a two-storey building with a shared central entrance.
There is double-glazing. Some more insulation and draught proofing is needed but this would be easy to do.
Elderly people live in the other 3 flats. All residents share a conservatory which looks onto a colourful garden.

House B – Bungalow

A one-storey, 2 bedroomed house. It would be straightforward to build a ramp and rails at the front to give easy access.
It has an overgrown garden, with many shrubs, that needs some work. There is a very pleasant garden summer-house for sitting in.
The bungalow is fully double glazed throughout and has full gas central heating. It is cheap to heat in the winter.

Using the information above, decide which house, **House A or House B**, would be the **better** choice for Millie Smith **to meet her needs**.
Give **two** reasons to support your decision.
You **must** link the information about Millie Smith to the house you have chosen.

(ES, 4 marks)

*When making an option choice it is **vital** that you link the information about the person or place, etc., to the source information. Failing to do this **will** mean you do not gain full marks.*

116

General answer

Here are sample answers for both house options.

> House A
> One reason why I feel house A would be the better choice to meet Millie's needs is because *it is a ground floor flat. This means there would be no stairs for Millie to climb. This would be a benefit to her as she has recently had a hip operation and finds it more difficult to move about.*
>
> Another reason for choosing house A is because the information about Millie says *she is starting to feel lonely after the death of her husband.* This house would be a better choice because *there are elderly people living in the other three flats, which would give her people her own age to talk to.*
>
> House B
> One reason why house B would be the better choice to meet Millie's needs is because the information says that *the house is fully double glazed and has full gas central heating, meaning the house is cheaper to heat in winter.* This would be a good thing for Millie as it says *she is starting to feel the cold more and more.*
>
> A second reason for choosing house B is because the house information says *there is a very pleasant summer house for Millie to sit in.* This would be a positive as it says that *Millie has always enjoyed having a garden.*

*For an option choice question like this one, you must make sure you give a reason for your house choice **AND** link it to the information about Millie. This has been done in **red** for you.*

*Try other **Option choice** questions from the Bright Red General Past Papers for Modern Studies.*

Support/oppose

This means exactly the same as agree/disagree, for/against.

Remember that when you support and/or oppose you are giving reasons to agree with and reasons to disagree with a statement that a person is making, i.e. providing arguments for and against what they have said. In this type of question you will always have a statement/view to base your answer on.

If answering a For and Against question, you have to find evidence, based on the sources, that is **FOR** one of the sentences they have said and you have to find evidence that is **AGAINST** the other sentence they have said.

Look out for

Sometimes you may be asked to give two reasons to support a view **or** two reasons to oppose a view.

Chapter 8 Enquiry Skills

General question (2008 Q3b)

Source 1:
Information about selected countries

Country	Average Income ($)	Life Expectancy (Years)
China	1,290	72
Japan	37,180	82
Russia	3,410	65
United Kingdom	33,940	79
United States	41,400	78

Source 2:
Percentage of children enrolled in primary school (2006)

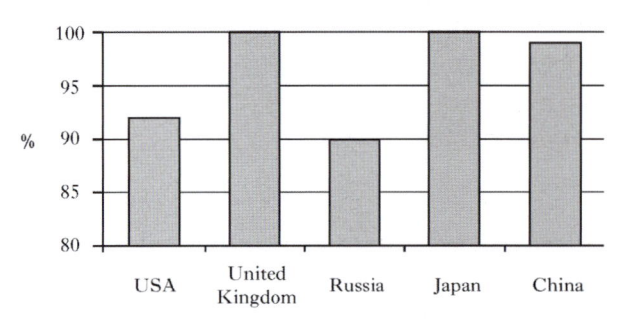

(Bar chart showing approximate values: USA 92%, United Kingdom 100%, Russia 90%, Japan 100%, China 98%)

The USA enrols less of its children in primary school than most other major countries. However, people in the USA have both the highest average income and live the longest.

View of Kelly Halcomb

Using **only** source 1 and source 2 above, give **one** reason to **support** and **one** reason to **oppose** the view of Kelly Halcomb.

(ES, 4 marks)

General answer

One reason to support the view of Kelly Halcomb when she says 'The USA enrols less of its children in primary school than most other major countries' comes from the evidence in source 2. It tells us that the USA enrols approximately 92% of its children in primary school. This is less than the UK and Japan with 100% enrolment. China has 98%, with only Russia having less than the USA.

One reason to oppose the view is when Kelly states 'people in the USA have both the highest average income and live the longest'. This is not true as, although they have the highest income with $41 400, $4220 more than Japan in second place, they do not live the longest. With 78 years, the USA is lower than people in Japan who live to 82 years on average.

In a Support/oppose General question, there will probably be only **two** sentences in the view or statement made by a person. One sentence will always be supported by one of the sources. The other sentence will always be opposed by the other source.

Make sure you notice the word 'both' in the second sentence. It is crucial you realise the view is directing you to Americans having **both** the highest income and living the longest. It is important you notice this because the sources do have one of these facts **BUT NOT BOTH OF THEM!**

You should always include the sentence from the view/statement that you are supporting or opposing in your answer. This makes the answer flow better and makes it easier for you to clearly provide the evidence.

!Look out for

Remember to make a comparison between evidence when answering Support/oppose questions. This will ensure you have full evidence to show that the statement/view is accurate or inaccurate.

Source evidence will always be present to back up your answer.

Try other **Support/oppose** questions from the Bright Red General Past Papers for Modern Studies.

Standard Grade Modern Studies

Exaggeration

When information is exaggerated it means it is not entirely true (it is inaccurate) or the truth has been stretched/overstated. As in support/oppose questions, exaggeration questions will have a statement or statements made by a person. They will say something and, using the evidence from the sources, you have to prove that what they are saying is exaggerated.

General question (2008 Q4d)

Study the Timeline below, then answer the questions which follow.

TIMELINE – NIGER FOOD CRISIS KEY EVENTS 2004–2006

Date	Event
August 2004	Hardly any rain falls during what should be the rainy season. The crops which do grow are then eaten by several plagues of locusts.
November 2004	There are appeals for aid. Many people run out of food.
January 2005	Foodstocks are very low. There is very little food for people to buy. People march in the streets to draw attention to the problem.
July 2005	All Niger's debt is cancelled at the G8 summit. This should help greatly. Many children are dying of starvation.
August 2005	800,000 children under 5 are still going hungry. 40,000 tonnes of energy biscuits are sent to Niger by Italy.
September 2006	The rain fails to come again. A quarter of the population are reported to be hungry.

Niger has suffered greatly due to a lack of rain. People in Niger protested about the situation. No food aid was received by Niger. Debt is still a major problem for the government.

View of Lyz Graham

Using **only** the information above, write down two statements made by Lyz Graham which are **exaggerated**.

Using the Timeline, give **one** reason why **each** of the statements you have chosen is **exaggerated**.

(ES, 4 marks)

This question is worded in two parts. However, you should treat it as a single question. Identify a statement (sentence) which is exaggerated (inaccurate) and provide evidence from the source which proves this.

Look out for

You should be continuing to look out for key words which are in bold or highlighted. These are prompts to ensure you answer **exactly** the way you are supposed to. If you don't carry out these prompts, you may not get full marks.

Chapter 8 Enquiry Skills

General answer

> One statement made by Lyz Graham which is exaggerated is when she says *'No food aid was received by Niger'*. We know this is exaggeration by her, as the timeline source says that *in August 2005, 40 000 tonnes of energy biscuits were sent to Niger from Italy*. This clearly shows that food aid has been received.
>
> A second statement which is exaggerated is when Lyz Graham states *'Debt is still a major problem for the government'*. This is exaggerated as the timeline shows that *in July 2005, all of Niger's debt was cancelled at the G8 summit*, therefore showing they no longer have any debt for it to be a major problem. *It was thought this would greatly help Niger.*

Try other Exaggeration questions from the Bright Red General Past Papers for Modern Studies.

Conclusion

Look out for

A conclusion style question is about looking at the trends of the source information (i.e. do figures increase or decrease over a period of time, do they alter between countries/areas, etc.). You **compare and contrast** source information.

You should be aware of the marking: 1 mark for identification and 1 mark for evidence. (Helpful if you are running out of time!)

Look out for

General Question (2008 Q4b)

The dates of the information and the numbers: are they in thousands, millions, etc.?

Data for selected NATO countries

Country	1990 Numbers in Armed Forces ('000s)	1990 Defence spending per person ($)	2005 Numbers in Armed Forces ('000s)	2005 Defence spending per person ($)
Greece	201	500	209	610
UK	308	770	216	530
USA	2,181	1,400	1,492	925
Turkey	769	110	816	115

Write down **two** conclusions about Armed Forces and Defence spending. You should write **one** conclusion with evidence about **each** of the following:
- The country with the biggest change in the numbers in its armed forces.
- What happens to the numbers in the armed forces as defence spending rises?

You **must** only use the information provided.

(ES, 4 marks)

This is now the style for General conclusion questions. You are prompted on where to focus your answer, which tends to help most candidates.

Look out for

Helpful tips in conclusion type questions. Answer on what it **prompts** you on!

Standard Grade Modern Studies

General answer

> One conclusion which can be made about the country with the biggest change in the numbers in its armed forces is, in the USA between 1990 and 2005, the numbers decreased by 689 000 members. This was the biggest change in comparison to the UK where numbers fell by only 92 000.
>
> A second conclusion which can be reached about the changes in the numbers in the armed forces as defence spending rises, shows that Greece saw an increase of 8000 in its forces between 1990 and 2005. This resulted in a spending rise to $610 per person in 2005 from $500 per person. Turkey also saw a rise in force numbers by 47 000; however their spending increased by only $5 per person.

If the biggest difference has been a **decrease**, you **must then compare** with another country where there is a **decrease**. DO NOT include a country where there is an increase.

Try other **Conclusion** questions from the Bright Red General Past Papers for Modern Studies.

Credit Enquiry Skills

Selective in the use of facts

In this type of question you should find evidence that may support or oppose the views that are given. There will be **three** statements within the view. You should look to see how much each statement within the view is either correct or incorrect.

You no longer need to draw conclusions about the degree of selectivity within each individual statement.

You decide whether each statement is correct or incorrect. At the end you decide overall how selective the view has been. You can have a situation such as:

- All 3 statements are correct = Not selective at all
- 2 correct, 1 wrong = Slightly selective
- 1 correct, 2 wrong = fairly selective
- All 3 incorrect = completely selective

You must reach an overall decision as to the level of selectivity. If you do not do this you will receive a maximum of 6 marks out of the available 8.

Look out for

Selective in the use of facts questions will be for 8 marks.

Chapter 8 Enquiry Skills

> **Look out for**
> Pay close attention to the titles and sources. They can be key to your understanding if a statement is correct or incorrect ...

Credit question (2009 Q1c)

Study sources 1, 2 and 3 below and on the next page, then answer the question which follows.

Source 1:
What should happen to Scotland after the 2007 Scottish Parliament Election Views of Main Parties

LIBERAL DEMOCRATS	LABOUR	CONSERVATIVE	SNP	GREENS
Increased powers for the Scottish Parliament but 'no' to independence	Scotland to remain in the United Kingdom	Scotland remains in the UK but willing to debate issues about devolved powers	Scotland to become independent after a referendum	Scotland to become an independent country

Seats in Scottish Parliament 2003 and 2007

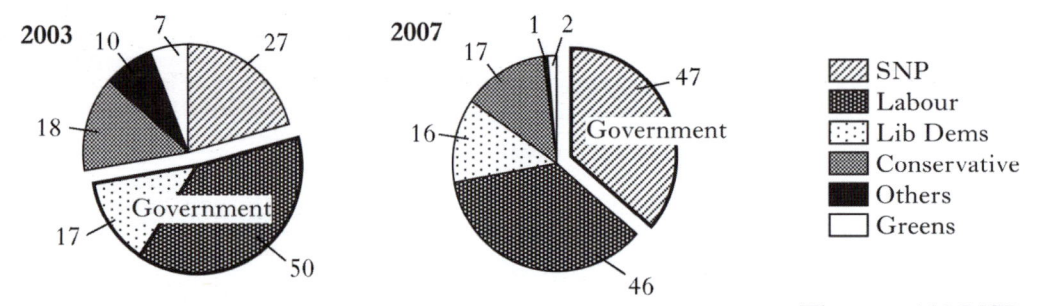

2003: 7, 10, 27, 18, Government 17, 50

2007: 1, 2, 17, 47 Government, 16, 46

Legend: SNP, Labour, Lib Dems, Conservative, Others, Greens

There are 129 MSPs

Source 2:
Scottish Parliament Elections (2003 & 2007) Regional Turnout

Region	Turnout 2003	Turnout 2007
1. Central Scotland	48·5%	50·5%
2. Glasgow	41·5%	41·6%
3. Highlands and Islands	52·3%	54·7%
4. Lothians	50·5%	54·0%
5. Mid-Scotland and Fife	49·7%	52·8%
6. North East Scotland	48·3%	50·7%
7. South of Scotland	52·3%	53·6%
8. West of Scotland	53·3%	56·5%
Scotland (Total)	49·4%	51·7%

Source 3: National Identity and the Scottish Parliament

People have different views on what makes a Scot. Is it supporting our football and rugby teams; is it a willingness to wear a kilt; is it a liking for traditional Scottish music or shortbread or the consumption of our national drink?

What makes a Scot?

A person's accent appears to be a very important factor when people are deciding if somebody is Scottish or not. A recent survey showed that 70% of Scottish people felt that a non-white person with a Scottish accent was Scottish whilst 54% believed that a person with an English accent living in Scotland, was not Scottish.

In 1999, prior to the opening of the Scottish Parliament, research carried out for the Government showed 25% of people in Scotland felt 'Scottish not British' and 11% said they would describe themselves as 'British not Scottish'. SNP voters and young people were much more likely to say they were Scottish whilst the elderly and Conservative voters were more likely to say they were 'British'. When the research was repeated in 2006, 32% of Scottish people said they would describe themselves as 'Scottish not British' and only 9% of those asked said that they were 'British not Scottish'.

The West of Scotland Region had the largest increase in voter turnout. In 2007, there were more MSPs in favour of independence than ever before and, since the opening of the Scottish Parliament, people feel more Scottish.

View of Callum Wishart

Using **only** sources 1, 2 and 3, explain **the extent to which** Callum Wishart could be accused of being **selective in the use of facts**.

(ES, 8 marks)

Credit answer

Callum Wishart is incorrect when he states 'The West of Scotland Region had the largest increase in voter turnout'. This is proven in source 2 which shows that the region saw a 3·2% increase in turnout. However, the Lothian region saw a 3·5% increase, clearly showing it had a higher increase than the West of Scotland. This shows Callum to be incorrect in his statement.

Callum is correct when he states 'In 2007, there were more MSPs in favour of independence than ever before'. The information to support Callum from source 1 shows that the number of MSPs favouring independence rose from 34 out of 129 in 2003 to 49 out of 129 in 2007. Therefore the evidence shows Callum to be correct in his statement.

Callum is also correct when he states 'since the opening of the Scottish Parliament, people feel more Scottish'. Source 3 supports this statement as it says in 1999, 25% of people said they felt more Scottish than British. This increased to 32% in 2006, an increase of 7%. This evidence shows Callum to be correct in his statement.

Overall Callum Wishart was correct in two statements and incorrect in one. Therefore he is slightly selective in his view.

Look out for

All three sources must be used in order to gain full marks.

Look out for

The statement and evidence are set in red to make it easier for you to identify the answer detail.

Chapter 8 Enquiry Skills

Credit question (2008 Q3c)

Study the information in sources 1, 2 and 3 below and on the next page, then answer the question which follows.

SOURCE 1

The Rockford Record
Your local voice, free to all 10 000 homes in Rockford City (23 May 2008)

New Housing Project Causes Local Anger
A recent public meeting in Rockford City Hall was attended by 500 local people. They were told about plans for a new gated community of 700 houses called 'Red Pines'. It is to be built by the Allan Building Company.
The gated community of Red Pines would be a walled housing development to which public access would be restricted. It would be guarded using CCTV and security personnel. The complex would have its own supermarkets, restaurants and bars.
The people at the meeting showed mixed feelings, for and against the possible development.
In 2004, gated communities housed 16 million Americans, about 6% of all households. Homeowners in gated communities live in upmarket and mostly white developments. Affluent black American homeowners are less likely than white people to live in gated communities.

The Red Pines Area Now
At the moment Red Pines is a beautiful wooded area. It is used by Rockford residents for walking and exercise. There is a jogging track, 3 football pitches and a rowing club on the river. Unfortunately, it floods occasionally as it is near to the river. Doctor Joan Quincy said, 'It is well known

Health and Exercise Statistics	Rockford	USA
Overweight	48%	35%
Bicycle riding	6%	16%
Exercise walking	16%	32%
Running/Jogging	4%	10%

that Rockford residents are not very good at taking exercise. Health statistics show that compared to the rest of the USA we need to take more exercise. We need the Red Pines area to keep our people healthy. We want to encourage more people to exercise in this area. Building houses would be a disaster for our community.'
The building of Red Pines would also cause a great deal of disturbance in and around the town. There might be a few short-term benefits for the local community but long-term, there will be no real gain for the town as those living in Red Pines are unlikely to be spending much money in the shops in Rockford. They will get in their cars and drive to the city which is only 15 miles away.
Doctor Quincy is also Chairperson of the Rockford Residents' Association.

SOURCE 2

What the people want
The Rockford Record decided to find out the views of local people about the 'Red Pines' development. We conducted an opinion poll and received 8900 replies from 10 000 homes and feel that this survey shows the real views of the people.

The Questions: How Important	Unimportant	Not very important	Important	Very important
is it that Rockford stays a racially mixed town?	20%	15%	25%	40%
a problem is jobs to the people of Rockford?	15%	25%	20%	40%
is the Red Pines area for exercise?	20%	10%	45%	25%

Ethnic origin of Rockford's Residents
Other 8%
White 32%
Hispanic 29%
Black 31%

124

Standard Grade Modern Studies

SOURCE 3

Leaflet from Allan Building Company

I am Chairman of the Allan Building Company and I was born in Rockford. I have stayed here all my life and want to do the best for Rockford. There is great demand for this type of housing from middle and upper income groups who would not live in Rockford because of their fear of rising crime there. We already have 500 new families from outwith Rockford, wanting to move into Red Pines whenever it is built. They are a mixture of young and old with an ethnic mix of 50% White, 25% Hispanic, 24% Black and 1% other groups.

Impact on Rockford

SHORT-TERM IMPACT	LONG-TERM IMPACT
• Skilled workers employed in the building of Red Pines. • Unskilled workers also needed. • Workers on-site spend money in local shops. • Building supply companies will increase trade.	• Unskilled jobs will be available, e.g. cleaners. • Jobs will be available in the new shops and restaurants. • Shops in Rockford will gain extra business from the new residents close-by. • Local shops have the opportunity to become suppliers to the new restaurants and bars which will open. • Flood prevention measures will stop flooding.

The Red Pines gated development will cause many problems for our health and change the ethnic mix of Rockford. It will bring few benefits to the people of Rockford.

View of Findlay Smith, Editor, The Rockford Record

Using **only** the information in sources 1, 2 and 3, explain, **in detail, the extent to which** Findlay Smith could be accused of being **selective in the use of facts**.

(ES, 8 marks)

Credit answer

An example of **one** paragraph is given below. This is not a complete answer.

Findlay Smith is correct when he states *'The Red Pines gated development will cause many problems for our health.'* The information to support this statement from source 1 informs that *Red Pines is currently used for walking and exercise.* This will be lost if the gated development goes ahead. Added to this, source 2 states, *70% of residents think Red Pines is important or very important for exercise.* Therefore it is an important issue for residents. This information shows Findlay to be correct in his statement.

Complete the rest of this answer. Complete for 'Red Pines development changing the ethnic mix of Rockford', and also for the statement that 'It will bring few benefits to the people of Rockford.' Remember to make an overall decision as to the level of selectivity.

Chapter 8 Enquiry Skills

Support/oppose

The instructions for a Credit support and oppose question are the same as those for a General version. Ensure that you provide evidence for and against the view that has been given. The key is to include evidence from the source. You must also make a comparison between information in the same source to show the reason why you support or oppose the view.

Credit question (2008 Q3b)

Study sources 1 and 2 below, then answer the question which follows.

Source 1: Average Personal Income Level Per Person in the 10 Wealthiest US States ($)

	2003	2004	2005
Colorado	34 500	36 000	37 500
Connecticut	42 000	45 400	47 500
Delaware	34 100	35 900	37 100
Maryland	37 500	39 200	42 000
Massachusetts	39 500	41 800	43 700
Minnesota	34 000	35 900	37 300
New Hampshire	35 100	37 000	37 800
New Jersey	39 600	41 300	43 800
New York	36 100	38 200	40 100
Virginia	33 700	35 500	37 600

Source 2: Income Distribution in the USA

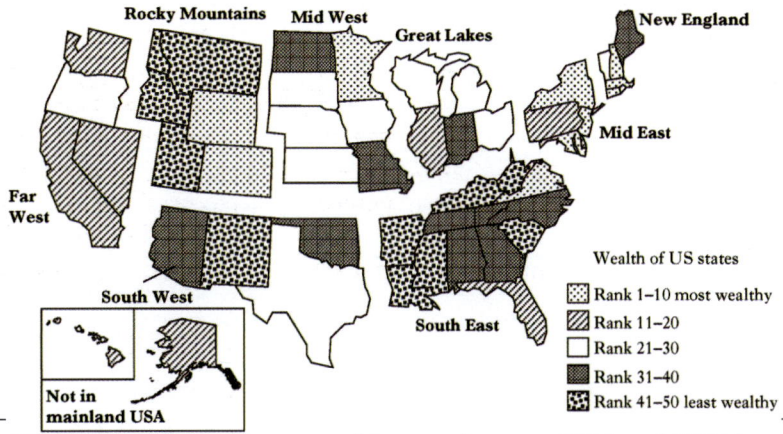

Map of USA showing regions: Rocky Mountains, Mid West, Great Lakes, New England, Mid East, Far West, South West, South East. Hawaii and Alaska shown as "Not in mainland USA".

Wealth of US states:
- Rank 1–10 most wealthy
- Rank 11–20
- Rank 21–30
- Rank 31–40
- Rank 41–50 least wealthy

> The biggest increase in personal income between 2003 and 2005 has been in Connecticut. The richest states in the US are all to be found in the Mid East of the country.
>
> View of a Wall Street Economist

Using only the information above, give **one** reason to **support** and **one** reason to **oppose** the view of the Wall Street Economist.

(ES, 4 marks)

You must make a comparison between the increase in Connecticut and an increase in another state to prove or disprove the view of the Wall Street Economist. You must also make a comparison between regions of the country for the second part of the answer.

Standard Grade Modern Studies

Credit answer

One reason to support the view of the Wall Street Economist is when he/she states *'The biggest increase in personal income between 2003 and 2005 has been in Connecticut.'* The evidence to support this view comes from source 1, where the evidence of US states wealth shows that the average personal wealth of Connecticut rose by $5500, from $42 000 in 2003 to $47 500 in 2005. This is the biggest increase, as the next largest is in Maryland where the increase was $4500. Therefore it is clear that Connecticut did have the biggest average increase.

One reason to oppose the view of the Economist is when he/she states *'the richest states in the US are all to be found in the Mid East of the country'*. This is inaccurate, as source 2 shows that although some of the ten richest states are in the Mid East, many are also to be found in the Rocky Mountains, Mid West, New England and South East. Therefore this clearly shows that not all the richest states are in the Mid East.

Look out for

Remember to make a comparison between evidence when answering support/oppose questions. This will ensure you have full evidence to show that the statement/view is accurate or inaccurate.

Conclusion

A conclusion style question is about looking at the trends of the source information (i.e. do figures increase or decrease over a period of time, do they alter between countries/areas, etc.). You **compare and contrast** source information.

The only significant difference between a General conclusion question and a Credit conclusion question is that at General you will be asked to make **two** conclusions. At Credit, however, it will **probably** be **four** conclusions in order to achieve 8 marks.

Look out for

At Credit level words such as 'relationship', 'commitment' and 'progress' will be used. Make sure you understand their meanings.

Chapter 8 Enquiry Skills

Credit question (2008 Q4c)

Study the information in sources 1, 2 and 3 below and on the next page, then answer the question which follows.

Source 1: Millennium Development Goals

The Millennium Development Goals were agreed by 189 countries in New York in 2000.

Selected Millennium Development Goals
1: **Reduce child mortality**
2: **Achieve primary education for all**
3: **Remove extreme poverty and hunger**
4: **Combat diseases**

These goals represented a commitment by rich and poor nations to expand social and economic progress in all regions of the world, as well as creating a global partnership for reducing levels of poverty and suffering in less developed countries by 2015.

Many are now questioning the commitment of the More Developed Countries to making these goals a reality as few MDCs give the UN recommended 0·7% of Gross National Income (GNI).

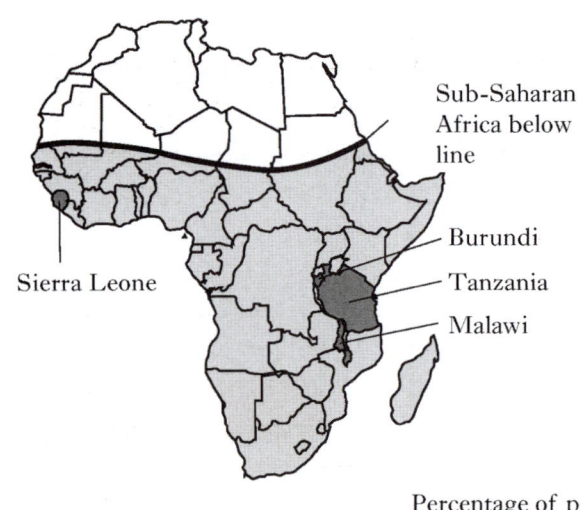

The World's Four Poorest Countries	
Average Income Per Person ($)	
1. Sierra Leone	490
2. Tanzania	523
3. Burundi	591
4. Malawi	615

Map labels: Sub-Saharan Africa below line; Sierra Leone; Burundi; Tanzania; Malawi.

Percentage of people living on less than $1 a day, 1995 and 2001

Bar chart showing Sub-Saharan Africa and All less developed countries for 1995, 2001, with a dashed 2015 target line.

Source 2: Aid given by selected Donor Countries

Selected Donor Countries	Aid Given 2004 $ billions (% of GNI)	2010 (prediction) $ billions (% of GNI)	% increase	Largest recipients ($ millions)
UK	7·88 (0·36)	14·60 (0·59)	85	1. India ($419) 2. Bangladesh ($267) 3. Tanzania ($265)
USA	19·7 (0·17)	24·00 (0·18)	22	1. Iraq ($2286) 2. Congo ($804) 3. Egypt ($767)
Portugal	1·03 (0·63)	0·93 (0·51)	−10	1. Angola ($367) 2. Cape Verde ($39) 3. Timor ($34)
Italy	2·46 (0·15)	9·26 (0·51)	276	1. Dem. Rep. Congo ($235) 2. China ($52) 3. Tunisia ($41)

Source 3

Four Poorest African Countries – Progress on selected Millennium Development Goals

Selected Indicators	Sierra Leone 1996	Sierra Leone 2006	Tanzania 1996	Tanzania 2006	Burundi 1996	Burundi 2006	Malawi 1996	Malawi 2006
% of population undernourished	44	50	50	44	63	67	50	34
Child Mortality (per 1000 births)	293	283	159	126	190	190	216	175
% 1 year olds vaccinated against measles	37	64	49	91	80	75	90	80
% Primary school enrolment	43	73	94	95	43	57	48	98

Using **only** the information on the previous page and above, you must **make** and **justify** conclusions about progress towards the Millennium Development Goals using the **four** headings below.
- Progress towards Millennium Development Goal 1
- Progress towards **all** of Millennium Development Goal 3
- The commitment of More Developed Countries to meeting the UN aid recommendation
- The commitment of Donor Countries to the world's **four poorest** nations

(ES, 8 marks)

Pay very close attention to the exact wording of the headings. This will help direct you to the correct source(s).

Chapter 8 Enquiry Skills

Credit answer

One conclusion which can be made about the progress towards Millennium Development Goal 1 is the aim of reducing child mortality rates has seen a reduction in this area. We can conclude this as in source 3 it states that child mortality per 1000 births has reduced in three out of the four poorest countries. For example in Sierra Leone the rate reduced from 293 in 1996 to 283 in 2006. Added to this the rate reduced in Tanzania by 33 and in Malawi by 41. Only Burundi saw no change, remaining at 190. This clearly shows that progress has been made.

A second conclusion which can be made regarding progress towards all of Millennium Development Goal 3 is that there has been limited success regarding the removal of hunger. This is shown in source 3 where the percentage of the population which is undernourished has dropped in only two out of four countries. Tanzania saw a 6% decrease in the number of undernourished, Malawi a 16% decrease from 50% in 1996 to 34% in 2006. This would therefore suggest some progress by some countries, but not others. Also there has been limited success in removing extreme poverty as source 1 states in Sub Saharan Africa the percentage of people having to live on less than $1 per day had risen from 42% in 1995 to 44% in 2001. This suggests progress has struggled in this area. However there had been an improvement among less developed countries generally as the percentage had fallen from 29% to just over 20% in 2001. This was showing an advancement towards the 2015 target of 15% of people living on less than this amount.

A conclusion regarding the commitment of More Developed Countries to meeting the UN aid recommendation is that little progress is being made. The UN suggests that MDC should give 0·7% of their Gross National Income. However source 2 shows that none of the selected donor countries give this amount. The UK has seen a slight increase between 2004 where it gave 0·36% and the predicted rate of 0·59% in 2010. Italy has shown some commitment to this aim as it has risen from 0·15% to 0·51%; however Portugal has actually shown a reduction in aid given. Their prediction for 2010 of 0·51% is down 0·12% from 2004. However, Portugal was very close to the recommendation in 2004, giving 0·63%.

A final conclusion as to the commitment of donor countries to the world's four poorest nations suggests a low level of commitment. Source 1 shows that Sierra Leone, Tanzania, Burundi and Malawi are the four poorest nations, with an average income of between $490 and $615 per person among these countries. A lack of donor country commitment is evident from source 2. This source shows that of the aid given by the UK, USA, Portugal and Italy, only Tanzania features once as a largest recipient. They gained $265 million dollars from the UK.

Remember, the relevant information in the answer is in red.

Option choice/decision making

Look out for

Option choice questions will be for 10 marks.

Credit question (2008 Q1c)

Study the Background Information about Gleninch and sources 1 and 2 on the next page, then answer the question which follows.

BACKGROUND INFORMATION ABOUT GLENINCH CONSTITUENCY

- Gleninch is a constituency in the north of Scotland with a population of 35 265 people. It is a largely rural area with only one town, Inverinch, and a large number of scattered villages. The traditional industries of farming and fishing have been in decline in recent years. The unemployment rate is well above the national average.
- Many young people leave the area, moving to the big cities throughout the UK to look for jobs or to attend college or university.
- Tourism is very important to the local economy, with a lot of people employed in hotels, bed and breakfast accommodation and restaurants. Tourists tend to visit the area for a few days on short breaks, attracted by rare wildlife and spectacular, unspoilt scenery. However, there are a number of transport problems in the constituency, including high petrol prices and poor public transport.
- There is a proposal to build a wind farm in the area. This would involve the construction of 6 large wind turbines along the coast, as well as a 15-mile long power line built on tall pylons to take electricity to the rest of the country. This would create a few temporary construction jobs but will disturb local wildlife and impact on the scenery of the area.
- An American mining company wants to build a huge 'super-quarry' into a mountainside near Gleninch. This will produce crushed rock to build roads, railways and houses throughout the UK. The new quarry will create 150 new jobs in Gleninch.
- At the last General Election, the constituency was won by the Labour Party with a majority of just over 1000 votes. The Liberal Democrats came second. They are convinced that, with the right candidate, they can win the seat at the next election.

A Statistical Profile of Gleninch Constituency (2006)

	Gleninch	Comparison with Scottish Average
Average Income	£21 185	–14%
Income Support claimants	15·1%	+22%
Unemployment Rate	5·6%	+13%
School leavers with no qualifications	3·6%	–33%
School leavers with Highers	58·6%	+13%
Serious Assaults	8·8 (per 10 000 people)	–73%
Housebreaking	3·8 (per 10 000 people)	–93%
Road Accidents	57 casualties	–44%

Survey of Local Liberal Democrat Members

Question: *How important are these issues to people in the area?*

Issue	Unimportant	Not very Important	Fairly Important	Very Important
Environment	5%	25%	40%	30%
Health	2%	10%	53%	35%
Jobs	0%	0%	48%	52%
Women in Parliament	15%	52%	22%	11%

There are two people hoping to be selected by the Liberal Democratic Party to be the Party's candidate at the next General Election. Here are extracts from speeches they have made.

SOURCE 1

EXTRACT FROM CAMPAIGN SPEECH BY KIRSTY REID

- I support the proposed wind farm as it will provide many local jobs and help the local environment.
- Our local schools provide an excellent education. If selected, I will work to ensure this continues.
- Women make up over half the country's population and yet there are still very few of us who are MPs. This is a major priority for local party members and is an important reason why I should be the candidate.
- The local economy has been in decline recently. We need more jobs to keep our young people in the area. The new quarry will help with this, and I will work hard to see that it is allowed to go ahead.
- To attract more people to the area we need to improve transport links. I will make this a priority.

SOURCE 2

EXTRACT FROM CAMPAIGN SPEECH BY ROBBIE McKAY

- Tourism is very important to the area and so I will oppose the new wind farm as it will be an ugly blot on the landscape and deter tourists.
- Crime in Gleninch is among the worst in Scotland. I will campaign to improve policing in the area.
- Although new jobs are important, local Liberal Democrats are much more concerned about the environment. The new quarry will put more heavy lorries on our roads which are already more dangerous than the rest of the country. I will oppose it going ahead.
- The issue of health will be one of my main concerns, just as it is for local party members.
- Compared to the rest of the country, the people of Gleninch are not well-off. I will do all I can to improve this.

Use **only** the information about Gleninch on the previous page and sources 1 and 2 above.

(i) State **which person** would be the **more suitable** to be selected by the Liberal Democratic Party as their candidate for this constituency at the next General Election.

(ii) Give **three detailed reasons to support your choice**.

(iii) Give **two detailed** reasons why you **rejected** the other candidate.

In your answer, you **must relate** information about the constituency to the information about the **two** candidates.

(ES, 10 marks)

Standard Grade Modern Studies

Answers must make explicit links between the background information about Gleninch Constituency **and** sources 1 and 2. You will be awarded 2 marks for doing this. Therefore if you do this for the **three** reasons why you chose the candidate you will receive 6 marks. If you also do this for the **two** reasons why you rejected the other candidate you will receive 4 marks. This will give you 10 marks in total.

Answers that do not make explicit links should be awarded 0 marks.

If you fail to explain why you rejected the other candidate you will be awarded a maximum of 6 marks.

Credit answer

Answer in support of Kirsty Reid as candidate

One reason to support Kirsty Reid as the Liberal Democratic Party candidate for Gleninch is, Kirsty says that she will work to ensure that the excellent education in the area continues. This is a good thing as the statistical profile of Gleninch shows school leavers with highers is 13% above the Scottish average. Therefore it is important this trend continues. Kirsty will aim to see this happens.

A second reason to support Kirsty is, she states, 'We need more jobs to keep our young people in the area. The new quarry will help with this, and I will work hard to see that it is allowed to go ahead'. This is an important issue as the background information about Gleninch states that 150 jobs will be created by the quarry. These new jobs will be important for the area. Kirsty will support this quarry development.

A final reason to support Kirsty is that the background information says 'there are a number of transport problems in the constituency, including high petrol prices and poor public transport'. Kirsty states she will make improving transport links a priority. This will help attract people to the area, making this a reason to select Kirsty.

One reason for rejecting Robbie McKay as the candidate for the Liberal Democratic Party is he believes 'Crime in Gleninch is among the worst in Scotland. I will campaign to improve policing in the area'. However this claim is disproved as the statistics show that crime in the area is quite low, with housebreaking 93% lower than the Scottish average, and assaults 73% lower. Therefore this suggests crime is not a major issue for Gleninch.

A second reason to reject Robbie is 'he opposes the new quarry because the local Liberal Democrats are much more concerned about the environment than jobs. Therefore I will oppose it going ahead'. However, this is not true. The survey of local party members shows that 52% think that jobs are very important, compared to only 30% for the environment. This suggests Robbie is wrong in his statement.

Use the same method to provide an answer supporting Robbie McKay as the candidate, and rejecting Kirsty Reid.

A good way to tackle an option choice question is to first read the introduction sentence next to the question number. This will give you an indication of what you are being asked to do. After doing this you should read the question, before the source information. Reading the question will give you a better idea of what to look for when you do then read the sources. When reading the sources it is a good idea to mark next to, or highlight, the information you think supports or rejects the person as the more suitable candidate.

Look out for
The statement and evidence are set in red to make it easier for you to identify the answer detail.

Look out for
Remember the 3:2 balance of arguments.

After you have completed an answer in support of Robbie McKay, try to answer the 2009, Credit paper Option Choice question, Ideologies section, question 3b, 10 marks.

Chapter 8 Enquiry Skills

Investigating/hypothesis

You will be asked at some stage in the ES section of the paper to answer an Investigating question. Do not worry! You are not being asked to do an investigation. You are only being asked to give the steps you would follow to go about completing an investigation if you were to work on one!

First we will look at a General example.

General question (2008 Q1c–e)

You are investigating the topic in the box below.

> CAMPAIGNING IN ELECTIONS

Answer questions (c), (d) and (e) which follow.
(c) As part of the **planning stage**, give **two** relevant **aims** for your investigation.

(ES, 2 marks)

Aims is another way of saying 'things you would want to find out' in order to complete the investigation topic which is in the box, i.e. things you want to find out related to 'campaigning in elections'.

General answer

An aim is something you are attempting to find out if you were carrying out the investigation.

The following aims would gain you 1 mark each.

- To discover/find out the main methods used by political parties, such as the SNP, when they are campaigning.
- To discover/find out which methods political parties have found to be the most useful.
- To discover/find out how parties decide which campaign method should receive the most resources.
- To discover/find out if high profile candidates/members make a difference to the level of interest in the campaigns.

*Remember the **aims** must be **relevant** to the topic.*

General question

You decide to contact some political parties to help with your investigation.
(d) Give **two** ways in which you could contact the political parties. For **each** way you have chosen, explain why it is a **good** way to get information to help in your investigation.

(ES, 4 marks)

! Look out for

Marking instructions will give you 1 mark for identification and 1 mark for explanation.

134

General answer
Ways of contacting parties/reason why it is a good way:

- Sending an e-mail to the party candidate. This is a good way of gaining information, as it allows appropriate questions to be asked quickly.
- You may wish to visit the local office of the party, such as the SNP office in Edinburgh. This is a good way, as it allows you to speak directly with officials and campaigners.
- You may choose to write a letter. This is a good way as it allows detailed questions to be asked about campaigning.

General question

You decide to use your local library to help with your investigation.
(e) Describe **one** way in which you could use your local library
(ES, 2 marks)

General answer
Ways in which you could use your library:

- Librarians are expertly trained in helping you find the exact information you are searching for.
- Many libraries, such as those in East Dunbartonshire, allow you to use the internet free of charge. This will allow you to search party websites and send e-mails to the political party.

Let's now study a Credit example.

A major difference between a General and Credit investigation is that at Credit level it requires you to include a **hypothesis**. A hypothesis is a statement relevant to the topic you are asked to study. It is a statement you develop that you can prove or disprove. The topic in the question we will study is about AIDS/HIV in Africa. For it to be a correct hypothesis it **must** be a statement. It **cannot** be a question. If you can put a question mark at the end of it then it is not a correct hypothesis!

What makes a good hypothesis?

Often people get confused with what a hypothesis is or even how you work out what a correct hypothesis is. There is a simple method you can use to make sure you come up with a relevant hypothesis!

Chapter 8 Enquiry Skills

It is called GART. GART has four elements.

G = Gender
A = Age
R = Race
T = Time

If you can produce a hypothesis (statement) based on one of these issues you will produce a correct hypothesis answer.

We will now see how GART can be used in the issue in the box, which we will also study in the next question. (Remember a hypothesis is a statement you can **PROVE OR DISPROVE**.)

HIV/AIDS in Africa

- It is possible to produce a hypothesis based on Gender. For example: More women than men suffer from HIV/AIDS in Ethiopia.
- It is possible to produce a hypothesis based on Age. For example: HIV/AIDS is more likely to affect younger people than older people in Sudan.
- It is possible to produce a hypothesis based on Race. For example: There is a higher rate of HIV/AIDS among black South Africans than there is among white South Africans.
- It is possible to produce a hypothesis based on Time. For example: Fewer Africans died of HIV/AIDS in 2009 than of the disease in 2008.

Remember this is a guide. GART is not an exhaustive way of producing a hypothesis. There are other ways, as detailed in the answer below part b.

Each of these hypothesis examples, based on GART, would receive 2 marks (full marks).

Credit question (2009 Q4 b–e)

You have been asked to carry out **two** investigations.
The first investigation is on the topic in the box below.

HIV/AIDS in Africa

Now answer questions (b) and (c) which follow.
(b) State a relevant **hypothesis** for your investigation.

(ES, 2 marks)

Credit answer

The following examples of a hypothesis would receive 2 marks.

- Improved education would help with the HIV/AIDS problems in Africa.
- HIV/AIDS is a growing problem in Africa.
- HIV/AIDS is a problem which receives little government support in South Africa.
- More women than men suffer from HIV/AIDS in Ethiopia.

This hypothesis example is not based on GART. These are other possible examples. There are lots you can use!

Standard Grade Modern Studies

Credit question

(c) Give **two** relevant **aims** to help you prove or disprove your hypothesis.

(ES, 2 marks)

Aims is another way of saying 'things you would want to find out' in order to complete the investigation topic which is in the box, i.e. things you want to find out related to HIV/AIDS in Africa, which will prove or disprove your hypothesis.

The following aims would gain you 1 mark each:

For the hypothesis: More women than men suffer from HIV/AIDS in Ethiopia.
- Aim to find out what the exact numbers are of women and men who suffer from the disease.
- Aim to find out if there has been a change in the numbers of women sufferers over a period of time.
- Aim to find out the level of aid given to Ethiopian women from the UK for those suffering from HIV/AIDS.

The second investigation is on the topic in the box below.

The benefits of EU expansion

Now answer questions (d) and (e) which follow.

(d) Describe, **in detail**, **two** factors that must be taken into account when designing and carrying out a survey.

(ES, 4 marks)

This means things you should consider when you are planning a survey.

A survey is a way you would find out people's opinions on a particular issue.

Credit answer

- You must consider the time of day you carry out a survey. At night you are likely to survey more people.
- The number of people you survey. You will gain a wider response from 500 people rather than 50 people.
- You must take care with the type of question asked. Closed questions give a YES or NO answer. You will gain less detail this way.

Chapter 8 Enquiry Skills

Credit question (2009 Q4 e)

(e) You also decide to carry out a search on the internet.

You enter the phrase 'Benefits of EU expansion' into an internet search engine.

Six results are shown below.

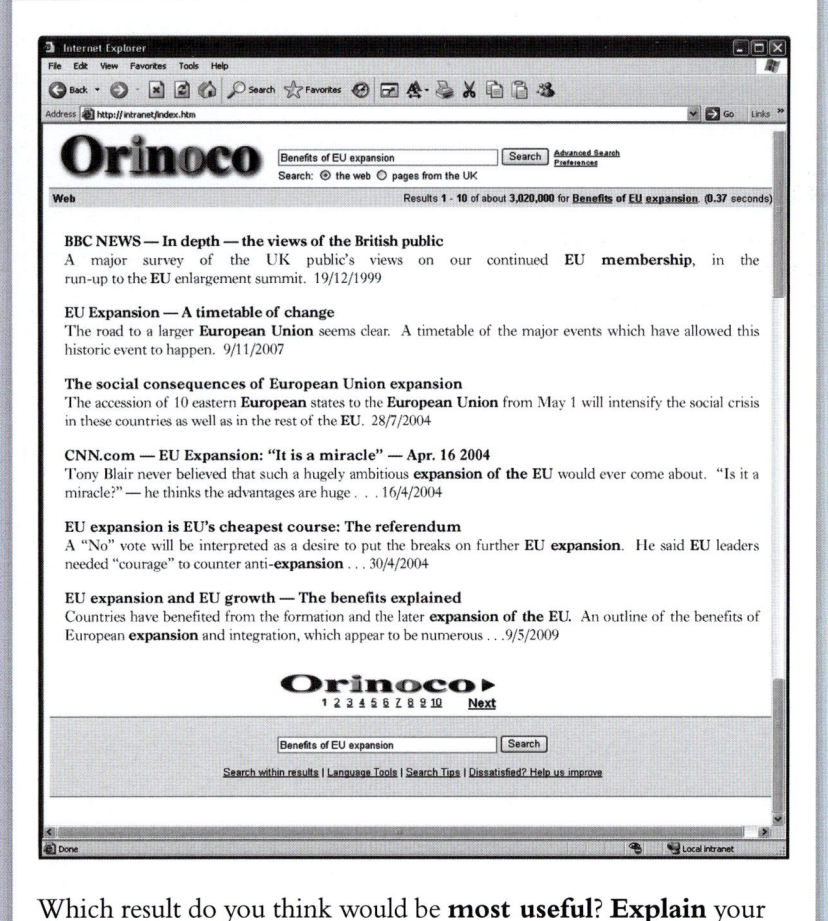

*Remember you are making a decision about which web link result would be most useful for the topic you are searching for: Benefits of EU expansion. Therefore you **must** focus on a result which includes the word benefits in its title.*

Orinoco

Benefits of EU expansion

Results 1 - 10 of about 3,020,000 for Benefits of EU expansion. (0.37 seconds)

BBC NEWS — In depth — the views of the British public
A major survey of the UK public's views on our continued **EU membership**, in the run-up to the **EU** enlargement summit. 19/12/1999

EU Expansion — A timetable of change
The road to a larger **European Union** seems clear. A timetable of the major events which have allowed this historic event to happen. 9/11/2007

The social consequences of European Union expansion
The accession of 10 eastern **European** states to the **European Union** from May 1 will intensify the social crisis in these countries as well as in the rest of the **EU**. 28/7/2004

CNN.com — EU Expansion: "It is a miracle" — Apr. 16 2004
Tony Blair never believed that such a hugely ambitious **expansion of the EU** would ever come about. "Is it a miracle?" — he thinks the advantages are huge . . . 16/4/2004

EU expansion is EU's cheapest course: The referendum
A "No" vote will be interpreted as a desire to put the breaks on further **EU expansion**. He said **EU** leaders needed "courage" to counter anti-**expansion** . . . 30/4/2004

EU expansion and EU growth — The benefits explained
Countries have benefited from the formation and the later **expansion of the EU**. An outline of the benefits of European **expansion** and integration, which appear to be numerous . . . 9/5/2009

Which result do you think would be **most useful**? **Explain** your answer.

(ES, 2 marks)

Look out for

When dealing with web link sources like those found in this question, a key way to discover which is the correct answer is to ensure the topic appears in the web link title. Also, make sure you look at the date of the link. The more up to date the web link the more likely it is to be the correct choice.

Credit answer

For the full 2 marks you **must** state which result would be the most useful **AND** give a reason to explain why this is the case.

The result which would be the most useful when searching 'Benefits of EU expansion' is 'EU expansion and EU growth – The benefits explained'. The reason for this is that it is the only result which contains the benefits of EU expansion. Added to this it has the most up to date material on the issue of the EU, posted in May 2009.

Other research methods

As well as internet searches and surveys, there are other research methods that can be asked about. You may be asked to give the benefits/advantages or problems of using the following as a way of researching:

- using the library to research
- writing letters to representatives
- e-mailing representatives.

Chapter 9 Conclusion

This book has taken you through a whole range of aspects of your Modern Studies course. It has explained concepts and their importance, the key need for correct and developed writing skills in Modern Studies, General exam and Credit exam papers, as well as the two elements of your course and examination, Knowledge and Understanding and Enquiry Skills.

This book has helped revisit and refresh the key KU aspects of each syllabus area and the topics within them. You have discovered skills in **properly** reading questions! Added to this you have found that there are not actually that many different types of questions, KU in particular, that you can be asked. Remember to pay close attention to the Look out for! boxes to give you tips on how to pick up those vital extra marks.

Among the most important features of this book are the examples included in the recap summary and the sample answers. Hopefully you have found them useful and please do use some of them. A weakness among many Modern Studies candidates is the lack of examples included in answers. Hopefully this book will have helped cure this! You can build up your own examples, though, by accessing some of the suggestions throughout the book. These newspapers, television stations and websites really are a great, easy and convenient way to find lots of useful and relevant examples.

Please remember, though, that this book is not everything! You need to put in the work. You must work hard, practise questions, revise your knowledge and challenge the opinions and ideas of the world that you study in Modern Studies. **DON'T EVER** be afraid to give your opinion in a class discussion or disagree with ideas in group work. Discussing and challenging our thoughts is possibly *the* best way of learning and developing your confidence. This will help you enormously in the world of Standard Grade Modern Studies.

I hope this book helps give you the confidence to push on from Standard Grade and move into Intermediate, Higher and beyond. Success in Modern Studies is a gateway to politics and the political world. One day you might just find yourself in Downing Street…!